living in a
grey world

rediscovering
the black and white
truth of the Word

living in a
grey world

A.J. Hawks

TATE PUBLISHING & Enterprises

Published by Tate Publishing & Enterprises, LLC
127 E. Trade Center Terrace | Mustang, Oklahoma 73064 USA
1.888.361.9473 | www.tatepublishing.com

Tate Publishing is committed to excellence in the publishing industry. The company reflects the philosophy established by the founders, based on Psalm 68:11,
"The Lord gave the word and great was the company of those who published it."

Book design copyright © 2009 by Tate Publishing, LLC. All rights reserved.
Cover design by Kellie Southerland
Interior design by Joey Garrett

Published in the United States of America

ISBN: 978-1-61566-401-6
1. Religion / Christian Life / General
2. Religion / Christian Life / Social Issues
09.11.24

Dedicated to the congregation of Evergreen
Christian Fellowship, whose lights on their new
building (Finally!) are only outshone
by their love for Jesus Christ.

Acknowledgements

Thank you to ...

My parents. Where would I be without them (both literally and metaphysically)?

Ceri Fox for both her invaluable input and her limitless wisdom provided when in most dire need.

Graham Briggs for his endless encouragement and inspiring dedication.

Scott Thayer for demanding the utmost of his students when most were content to just live on Sundays.

Monte Montemayor for forging a heart within my chest that to this day yearns for truth.

Angela Muscat and Andrew Hwang for being friends in a world full of acquaintances.

Jessie Schubert for being the spiritual sandpaper I so often needed.

Daniel Jackstadt for reminding me why it is that we do what we do.

And to God, the light in my darkness.

Table of Contents

Foreword   **11**

Dear Reader   **15**

The Mystery of the Lost Keys   **21**

The Bible as We Know It (Supposedly)   **25**

Hello? Is Anybody Listening?   **41**

Sex Outside of Marriage   41

Sex Outside of Marriage (In Your Head)   44

Potty-Mouth Syndrome   47

Gossiping   50

Unequally Yoked   53

Drugs/Alcohol   57

" … It's the Law"   61

America's Idols   63

Lying (And Yes, White Ones Count Too)   65

Homosexuality   68

Gambling 71

Divorce 73

The Pack 10 76

The Contemplative Lifestyle 78

Garbage in, Garbage ... Well, You Know 86

Teeth Whitening and Jesus **91**

What is Love? **107**

A Life Worth Living **117**

Foreword

The reader of this book does well to take heed of the author's warning, which states, "be prepared for an abrasive and sarcastic tone." He forgot to add painful, harsh, thorny, and controversial. You may be asking yourself why you should spend your valuable time reading such a book when you could be spending that time in a normal self-indulgent and cosset existence. That is the very point of the author's work. He boldly squares off against the norm that he finds so prevalent in his generation. He writes directly to his peers in the post-modern, easy believeism, egocentric Christian community who have lost their ability to apply biblical truth to their real lives. His generation is replete with head knowledge and is emaciated with heart knowledge. This community is like many who have come before, who have attempted to bring biblical thinking and worldly thinking into holy matrimony. When biblical truth is pitted again worldly wisdom, which do you suppose will be compromised?

> If the foundations are destroyed, what can the righteous do?
>
> Psalm 11:3

All it takes is to think a simple thought: "The Bible doesn't really say what it says." In other words, one simply imagines, "God didn't really mean that." What happens then when an entire generation thinks as such? We find a generation of people who have lost their appetite for truth. In fact, the taste of truth becomes bitter. Taking this one step further: what happens when one of their own begins to address these issues? I am not going to compare this author to Luther or Constantine, but like anyone who goes against the accepted religious norm, he places himself in harm's way. And so may the reader of this book who takes heed to the truths and principles presented in this treatise.

The author's topics are relevant to the issues faced by the modern Christian but not unlike those faced by those who have come before us. Satan has always been an equal opportunity tempter and is quite good at finding the issue specific to his prey. The reader will no doubt stumble upon a chapter pertaining to a personal issue that is directly addressed by the author. It may be tempting to fast-forward to a less invasive chapter, but I encourage you to hear him out. You should expect it to sting you as it stung did me. But in the midst of me defending, back peddling, and justifying my sinful black heart, I find scriptural support for his arguments.

To the author, I write "thank you and well done." I am looking forward to the next version, which should be written in fifteen years. By then you will have been knocked around a bit and have a few scrapes and bruises. You will be better at sinning because you'll have more experience doing it. You will also have a deeper understanding of grace. The words that you have written will be as true then as they are now but they will come alive with the reality of God's love, mercy, and forgiveness.

P. "Monte" Montemayor
February 15, 2009

Dear Reader

It has been quite a journey that has brought this book to your hands. To be honest, I can't entirely explain what compelled me to write this other than to say God. I really don't know.

Following my time teaching at Evergreen Christian Fellowship, I began to reflect on my unique experience there. After my time, I had gone through fifteen sermons, an eight-week series on apologetics, and a winter camp. I say this, not to brag, but to pause and just say, "Wow." I am so blessed to have had that incredible opportunity as a high school student. I mean really, how often do people get that chance? God has, in my life, surrounded me with people who have encouraged me and been a blessing beyond words, and I can do nothing but thank God for that.

God speaks to the people of Israel about his plans saying:

> "For My thoughts are not your thoughts,
> Nor are your ways My ways," declares the Lord.
> "For as the heavens are higher than the earth,
> So are My ways higher than your ways
> And My thoughts than your thoughts."

> Isaiah 55:8–9

I can think of nothing better to explain the opportunities my life has been given. I could spend all day asking, "Why me?" But it wouldn't amount to anything. So, I turned instead to asking, "What have I been communicating this whole time?" And I started to write. The culmination of that thought process is now in your hands.

My message is not a nice one. It, as you will hopefully see, is not comfortable. It is my hope, however, that you will see it for what it is: true. First, this is specifically written to Christians. If you are not and have this before you, I welcome you and encourage you to continue, but keep that fact in mind.

If you are reading this and know me, be prepared for vintage A.J. If you don't, be prepared for an abrasive and sarcastic tone. I did my best to avoid hiding my voice because I want to communicate with you in all honesty.

You may wonder whom specifically I am writing to. I'm writing to my generation and anyone who feels like the church has hid behind soft language and emotional pillows for far too long. The message of Christianity is radical and convicting. I intend to present it in such a way. If you are sensitive, again, I apologize. This may seem too harsh to you.

My proclamation of certain things as wrong is not to say I am above them. Rather, it is to serve as a statement of fact. I am not above these things that have been discussed, and in fact, in many cases, these are as much a confession of the state of my heart as they are the casting of judgment upon the church. I include myself in the verdict. And the verdict is guilty.

To maintain the veracity of my statements, I have included a ton of scripture. Hopefully, it will help. In case you were wondering, all the verses included (unless otherwise marked) are from the New American Standard Bible, chosen for its most literal translation, an approach I attempted to apply to my commentary as well.

Also, the middle section contains a series of examples of sinful behaviors, emphasizing the overall point that on moral issues where we seem to find grey, the Bible, in fact, leaves no room for such ambiguities. One of my goals in writing them was to maintain brevity in language to stick to the clear-cut nature of my message. Although I encourage you to take a look and read all of them, feel free to turn to the ones that specifically relate to you, should any of the issues presented be personally irrelevant.

Ultimately, I hope to make clear that Christianity is not just a life of happiness and contentment, but it is a life of joy, and there is a fundamental understanding in that statement that is critical to the Christian walk. I cannot emphasize enough the importance of our mission as Christians to live a life of worship. Too often Christianity devolves into this armchair religion where we talk about our salvation and don't get up and do something about it.

This is a call to arms, so to speak. It is time for Christians to get up off their comfy couches and start playing hardball. My prayer is that you will be convicted to serve our Lord Christ faithfully and with a sense of purpose until the coming of the kingdom.

Your brother,
A. J. Hawks

Therefore you have no excuse, everyone of you who passes judgment, for in that which you judge another, you condemn yourself; for you who judge practice the same things. And we know that the judgment of God rightly falls upon those who practice such things. But do you suppose this, O man, when you pass judgment on those who practice such things and do the same yourself, that you will escape the judgment of God? Or do you think lightly of the riches of his kindness and tolerance and patience, not knowing that the kindness of God leads you to repentance? But because of your stubbornness and unrepentant heart you are storing up wrath for yourself in the day of wrath and revelation of the righteous judgment of God, who will render to each person according to his deeds: to those who by perseverance in doing good seek for glory and honor and immortality, eternal life; but to those who are selfishly ambitious and do not obey the truth, but obey unrighteousness, wrath and indignation. There will be tribulation and distress for every soul of man who does evil, of the Jew first and also of the Greek, but glory and honor and peace to everyone who does good, to the Jew first and also to the Greek. For there is no partiality with God. For all who have sinned without the Law will also perish without the Law, and all who have sinned under the Law will be judged by the Law; for it is not the hearers of the Law who are just before God, but the doers of the

Law will be justified. For when Gentiles who do not have the Law do instinctively the things of the Law, these, not having the Law, are a law to themselves, in that they show the work of the Law written in their hearts, their conscience bearing witness and their thoughts alternately accusing or else defending them, on the day when, according to my gospel, God will judge the secrets of men through Christ Jesus.

Romans 2:1–16

The LORD is slow to anger and abundant in loving-kindness, forgiving iniquity and transgression; but he will by no means clear the guilty, visiting the iniquity of the fathers on the children to the third and the fourth generations.

Numbers 14:18

"The Word is the mirror in which we see Christ and, seeing him, are changed into his likeness by the Holy Spirit. If the glass is cracked, our conception of him will be distorted, whereas the Word in its native clearness sets Christ out in all his glory."

—William Gurnall,
The Christian in Complete Armour

The Mystery of the Lost Keys

Have you ever been looking for something you seem to have misplaced? Of course you have. My guess is, like everyone else, you've realized that your keys, phone, or who knows what, is gone. You simply don't know where it is. Immediately your mind flies to the least likely places it would be. Your mind races with questions. Where did I leave it? What did I last do with it? How am I supposed to find my phone when it's on vibrate?

Now, sometimes these situations really are complicated and impossible to solve, but how many of those times have you searched for hours, only to find it sitting in the most obvious "under your nose" place? How many times have your keys been sitting in the car while you ran around the house like the world was falling apart, yelling at your family to help, and simultaneously feeling like killing someone? Then, after hours of tear-your-hair-out frustration, you realize you haven't checked the car.

The question I want to pose is: Why wasn't the car checked first? I know, the question is obvious, and it's the same question you ask yourself when you realize the keys were in the car all along. So often in life, things happen that we overdramatize and turn into this huge, tragic, life-changing debacle, almost like we want the complicated solution. Sometimes, I think we are so intent on looking for the "grey" areas in life that we miss the clearly established black and white situations. If we knew as a fact that a line was straight, it would be pointless to look for ways to ensure that it was straight. And yet often, as Christians, we know what is right, but nonetheless, spend endless hours looking for ways to ensure that it's right.

Now, let's establish some groundwork before this is explored more fully. If you are reading this, the assumption that underscores this entire book is that you are Christian. If you indeed believe that Jesus is the Son of God and that he died to redeem mankind of our insurmountable sins so that we could again have the option to be reunited with the Creator, then you assume Jesus speaks the truth, yes? If Jesus lied, he wouldn't be much of a sinless man to die for us. Exodus 20:16 reads, "You shall not bear false witness." If Jesus couldn't even keep one of the basic tenets of God's law, how exactly could he serve as the *perfect* sacrifice? He couldn't! Thus, we as Christians assume that Jesus was the perfect Son of God, and we secondly must assume that he never lied.

Since he never lied, he obviously was telling the truth when he preached or made any statement whatsoever. Now, the only other option is that he thought he was telling the truth, but in all actuality was mistaken. Of course, this violates the assumption that he is the Son of God. The gospel of John describes Christ saying this:

> In the beginning was the Word, and the Word was with God, and the Word was God. He was in the beginning with God. All things came into being through him, and apart from him nothing came into being that has come into being. In him was life, and the life was the Light of men.

> John 1:1–4

In the above passage, John uses the term "the Word" to clearly refer to Jesus, given the context. It also would evoke to Hebrew readers a sense of creation and to a Greek it would evoke a principle that governed everything. From this, a huge amount of information on John's message about the nature of Jesus can be gained, but it primarily provides an obvious response to the suggestion of an accidental ignorance on Jesus' part. Does the man from the above passage sound like an ignorant person? My thought is no. Continuing on, then, we have assumed that he is indeed the Son of God, and that everything he says is true. That in itself packs quite a punch if we really think about the all-inclusive nature of these assumptions.

In John 10:35, Jesus says something immensely interesting, which by itself makes a huge impact on the nature of the Word of God. He says, "The Scripture cannot be broken." In Mark 13:31, Jesus says, "Heaven and earth will pass away, but my words will not pass away." Although slightly different, they both make the same point. All of Scripture is collectively eternal. Its truths are always true, and its commands are always going to be, well, commands. Isaiah 40:8, which according to Jesus is true and eternal, says: "The grass withers, the flower fades, but the Word of our God stands forever." Get the point?

Thus far, we have three core assumptions. First, as a Christian, you believe that Jesus is the Son of God. Second, as the Son of God, he always tells the whole truth, free of ignorance. Third, because he said that it was so and he always tells the truth, the Bible is eternally true and undeniably without flaw. It is upon these assumptions that the rest of this book is built.

The Bible as We Know It (Supposedly)

In case you haven't looked recently, the Bible is really quite long. Not even kidding. My guess is you haven't, at least in a long while, looked at the huge book sitting on the coffee table and thought, "Wow. That is absolute truth that I need to absorb and apply to my life, drastically changing everything I do and saving me a ton of heartache." Come to think of it, I don't actually know if I've ever thought that (at least in those exact, rather excessive words). Now, since it is really long and full of truths to be learned, you can imagine that it is actually a rather useful book. Timothy says this as to the scriptures:

> All scripture is inspired by God and profitable for teaching, for reproof, for correction, for training in righteousness; so that the man of God may be adequate, equipped for every good work.
>
> 2 Timothy 3:16

It basically says the Bible is perfect and therefore useful for all sorts of learning processes.

Think of it kind of like this: picture a man who for some reason or another was never introduced to society. He has no idea of traditional societal rules or any form of tact whatsoever. Yet, he is rather comfortable in his ignorance, without any real worries. After all, he has no idea what he's missing. Suddenly, he is told that he will have to be introduced to society and is handed an enormous book labeled "Society: How to Live Properly." Obviously, this book would be a huge asset to the man and certainly aid him in his life. After all, a man who wears a dress will not get very far in professional business, regardless of his skills. Yet, he faces a choice. Either he can spend a large part of his life reading the manual to figure things out, or he can choose to ignore his limiting ignorance. Granted, he doesn't actually know firsthand why he needs these skills, nor can he imagine the consequences. He simply knows that the manual says that consequences do indeed exist. Now, a cynical man (which, frankly, most of us are) might opt to test out life for a day or two just in order to verify that the manual and all the tedious studying associated with it is actually necessary. And who could blame the man? It is, after all, a very big book.

Now, this first day, he goes into the world and makes a minor mistake, such as not holding the door open for someone. It's rude and annoying, but people will get over it. So, he continues as he is and ignores his monstrous encyclopedia. He will probably repeat this mistake. Who, after all, would say something if the door wasn't held open? As he continues with his routine, day after day, he makes more mistakes. Some he learns from, and others he is never aware of committing. His uncorrected mistakes add up to create a rather selfish, generally disliked man who is known for his lack of tact and impoliteness.

Of course, the improvements he notes make *him* think he's doing just fine. Alas, he is the farthest from fine. Picture if this were to continue indefinitely, with both corrected and unaddressed mistakes occurring as he goes, until eventually he is nothing but the dregs of society. Tragic, to be sure. He likely would spend many of his days wondering: *Just what went wrong, exactly?* Some of his mistakes were probably big. After all, expressions of unwanted sexual interest in the work place are apparently frowned upon by most of society.

One night, out of curiosity, he looks at the manual briefly, and discovers that sexual advances are unacceptable in a professional atmosphere. The realization strikes him like lightning. If he had read this book, he wouldn't have been fired with a restraining order and a pending court date.

As a spectator, you may be looking in the fishbowl of this man's life and thinking that he is a complete fool. He is. There can be no debate. Here he has a book that says exactly what he should do to make everyone like him—and even some tips on successful business practices—and he ignores it. Can we really feel pity when he makes a mistake that he easily could have known to avoid? Even if we could, should we? What would that say about our standards? Rather, it would imply that we ourselves have little or none (albeit, this may be the case, but I digress). Even worse would be if he had read the manual and made the mistake anyway. How foolish would he look if he had already read that he should open the door for people and say "please" and "thank you" or he would be seen as rude, and yet he ignores this in favor of seeing what people actually think? Since he knows *as a fact* that this manual is absolutely true, does he not look infinitely stupid?

Now, back to his sexual assault. This book says clearly that he shouldn't have done that or he would be sent to court and arrested. Granted, he may not have read this part. But say that he had. Say that this part was one of the "big ones" that everyone knew about. You know, those general "isms" that pop culture of fifty years ago have made a permanent part of the world. Even worse, imagine that the man who gave him the book, advising him not to do these crimes, is also now his judge. Imagine the embarrassment that would be associated with this. Now picture the judge leaning across the table asking a simple question, "*Why in the world* did you do that? I told you to read the book, which said specifically not to make unwanted sexual advances on women or you would be punished. Did you not believe me that it was true?"

"Well … umm … no, that is, you see … I do believe it, entirely. I know it's true."

"All right. Then what happened?"

"Well … I … well … " And then here it comes—the inevitable excuse, right? Everyone has *some* excuse. There are plenty available. He could go the "I needed to experience it" route. Or perhaps he'll choose the "It's complicated" option. Or maybe even the "I couldn't help it" express. The judge, at this point, leans back, shakes his head, and gives a "You're an idiot" look for the ages. The judge, of course, apologizes out of courtesy (something you could learn from the book) and says he still has to punish the man because, frankly, there is no justifying an action he knew was wrong.

Of course, the man is shocked. *You mean, I'm being punished for doing something I know I shouldn't have and was warned by the lawmaker that it was wrong? How is that fair?* Oh, wait. It is.

Now, as for his excuses. The first is easily done away with. He says he felt the need to experience it? Really? It was a *necessity* that compelled him to sexually advance on a woman in the work place? Or maybe he needed to do it so that he could know for himself that it was a bad thing. Why? If he honestly knew and believed that the manual he was given was true, then *why in the holy potluck* did he need to experience it, given that the manual said it was bad? I have heard that shooting one's self hurts, but I've never done it. Should I do it just so that I "know for a fact" that it is indeed a rather painful affair? Obviously no. This leaves us with only two options. Either he doesn't actually believe that the manual is true (which is a completely separate issue), or he *wanted* to do what he did, despite the self-recognized fact that the manual was indeed true. This of course implicates the criminal even more because that means he willingly and in full knowledge chose to disobey the law. He may choose to argue that it's more complicated, and at last, we arrive at the grey area. Why is it more complicated? Picture the conversation.

"It's complicated."

"How so?"

"Well, you don't know what I was feeling inside. It was powerful, and there are a ton of emotional considerations here. I *couldn't* just not do it."

"How is it complicated? I said, 'Don't do that.' Did that confuse you or something? I didn't, quite frankly, ask if you felt emotional about it. Your feelings are irrelevant to whether it's right or wrong. I just said, 'Don't.'"

"Yes, but it was a really powerful feeling, an incredible force that compelled me."

"So you wanted to do it?"

"Yes … I mean … no … "

"You didn't want to, but you were compelled to do it?"

"I … you don't know how hard it was."

"First off, you keep assuming that I don't know what it was like, but remember when I gave you the manual, I also spent time as a normal person. I've been there, done that. I do know. So stop with the whole teenage girl, 'You don't understand what I'm going through!' thing. It's not helping your case. And secondly, the fact that it was hard means you wanted to do it. So no more, 'I didn't have a choice' out of you. So, if I do know what you are going through and you did indeed want it, that leaves me no choice but to assume that you chose to violate the law you knew about ahead of time (or at least could have known about ahead of time, if you chose to). Unfortunately, that leaves me no other option. You are guilty."

The above conversation actually addresses the second two excuses in one fell swoop. The judge makes the point that there isn't anything really complicated here. He knows it's hard. He didn't ask. He said, "Do this, don't do this, and I'll help. Any questions? No? Good." And the foolish man who chose to ignore him for his own pleasure, regardless of how he justifies it, has to be punished. After all, what would happen to the legal system if we started to make exceptions for people who "had a hard time" or "really wanted to do it"? What kind of court would listen to a thief who said, "Your Honor, I really, really, reeeaallly wanted it. I couldn't resist," and respond with a pat on the back, a sympathy hug, and a "you're off the hook" smile? The courts would get nothing done. Now, this is not to say that the judge holds no empathy for the accused. Indeed, he may hold a personal connection to the aforementioned idiot because he forewarned him (which would imply an interest in the man's success), but the fact that the judge likes the criminal and knows that emotions are powerful does not change the moral and legal stipulations of the law.

Hopefully, the connections in the above metaphor to Christianity and (most) Christians today are obvious. As Christians, we have this book, which we assume is true because the Son of God said it was so, and we know that it therefore presents absolute truth. And yet, we continuously mess up and then justify it like the less-than-cultured man above did. Oftentimes, it works for easing our indigestion after a big sin that we know was wrong. How easy is it to simply say, "It's complicated" and leave it at that? How easy is it to tell ourselves that we are fighting this struggle that fogs up the windows? Suddenly, when we are convinced that we aren't entirely to blame, we feel better. We can continue what we are doing because maybe we are learning about life from the experience, or maybe it's simply too hard to stop. I mean, after all, it feels really good doing it. This train of thought goes all the way back to the garden. You know, that little instance that unraveled our nature as humanity for eternity? It goes like this:

> Now the serpent was more crafty than any beast of the field which the LORD God had made. And he said to the woman, "Indeed, has God said, 'You shall not eat from any tree in the garden'?" The woman said to the serpent, "From the fruit of the trees of the garden we may eat; but from the fruit of the tree which is in the middle of the garden, God has said, 'You shall not eat from it or touch it, or you will die.'" The serpent said to the woman, "You surely will not die! For God knows that in the day you eat from it your eyes will be opened, and you will be like God, knowing good and evil." When the woman saw that the tree was good for food, and that it was a delight to the eyes, and that the tree was desirable to make one wise, she took from its fruit and ate; and she gave also to her husband with her, and he ate. Then the eyes of both

of them were opened, and they knew that they were naked; and they sewed fig leaves together and made themselves loin coverings. They heard the sound of the Lord God walking in the garden in the cool of the day, and the man and his wife hid themselves from the presence of the Lord God among the trees of the garden. Then the Lord God called to the man, and said to him, "Where are you?" he said, "I heard the sound of you in the garden, and I was afraid because I was naked; so I hid myself." And he said, "Who told you that you were naked? Have you eaten from the tree of which I commanded you not to eat?" The man said, "The woman whom You gave to be with me, she gave me from the tree, and I ate."

Gen 3:1-12   Genesis 3:1–12

It's a funny thing to me, how little this story is actually reflected on. The nature of temptation and sin are things that are discussed consistently as part of the Christian lifestyle. The understanding of one's sinful nature is clearly critical to salvation. Yet this passage often doesn't come up. But there are some key things in this passage that are incredibly potent when considered and have obvious parallels to today (aside from the whole, oh, I don't know, "fall of mankind" thing).

So, what literally happens here? We have Eve approached by the serpent, attempting to convince her to eat the fruit from the tree God had strictly forbidden, to whom she eventually complies, proceeds to give it to her husband, and well, the rest is history. But what I think is especially interesting is how Satan convinces her to sin for the first time. He tells her, "You surely will not die! For God knows that in the day you eat from it your eyes will be opened, and you will be like God, knowing good and evil." Satan takes something she thinks is bad, makes it appear good, and then explains why *God* would have an interest in making it appear bad. *He explains why it is good.*

I think that is so incredibly indicative of how we suffer temptation! Take for example, the issue of homosexuality (which is explored further later). Here we have this thing that seems to be clearly explained as sinful, but we notice all of these other things such as how happy they can be. We raise objections along the lines of allowing people to be who they really are, not having to suppress their identity. We argue often that it is better for them to be faithful in homosexual marriage to one partner than to have many. In any case, what happens is that the line between right and wrong becomes blurred. All of a sudden, good and evil aren't so clear anymore. How important doctrine must be if it is so clearly and blatantly attacked by the great tempter.

Emphasizing this point is what Eve does next. She proceeds to provide her own reasoning, indicating that perhaps she wasn't quite convinced it was proper but that she did desire to eat the fruit. So she enhances the work the devil had already done. She allows herself to become confused.

How often have we felt like that as Christians? We *used* to know God was opposed to something, but then all of these benefits on the contrary present themselves, and suddenly, we are unsure and unwilling to commit to a set standard, to a firm stance on doctrine, even if it is clearly God ordained. Then, when God calls us out, we excuse ourselves in some clever (or not so clever) way. We justify with a whole plethora of excuses.

Christianity doesn't allot for grey areas in our lives. It is a cold cut, clearly defined thing that says, "This is wrong; this is right. Do good, and you will be blessed. Do evil, and you will be punished." It is not some intricate web of confusion and emotion. It's black and white. There is no mixing. None at all. Over and over again, the Bible makes the point that you can't be friends with both. In describing Jesus, the Apostle John says, "He was in the world, and the world was made through him, and the world did not know him" (John 1:10). Similarly, Paul warns the Corinthian church:

> Do not be bound together with unbelievers; for what partnership have righteousness and lawlessness, or what fellowship has light with darkness? Or what harmony has Christ with Belial, or what

has a believer in common with an unbeliever. Or what agreement has the temple of God with idols? For we are the temple of the living God; just as God said, "I will dwell in them and walk among them; and I will be their God, and they shall be my people. *Therefore, come out from their midst and be separate*," says the LORD. "And do not touch what is unclean; And I will welcome you. And I will be a father to you, And you shall be sons and daughters to me," says the LORD Almighty (Emphasis mine).

2 Corinthians 6:14–20

The passage above makes a pretty clear case. Our bodies are temples of the living God, and we are to live as such. The light cannot be one with the dark. There is either one or the other. As Christians, we have to understand that we cannot just ignore biblical truth. Peter commands the church:

As obedient children do not be conformed to the former lusts which were yours in your ignorance, but like the Holy one who called you, be holy yourselves also in all your behavior because it is written, "You shall be holy, for I am holy."

1 Peter 1:14–16

Call me crazy, but I see very little suggestion in the above passage. I see an order. I wonder, why is it that we don't see it like that anymore? Why do we not hear the Creator of the universe? We have this vision nowadays of a kind, loving, forgiving God that cares for us and wants us to be happy above all else. We love to think about the happy things about God, the aspects that make us feel good about our lives and ourselves. He's merciful, understanding; he can relate, and he wants to be with us. We ignore the parts that don't leave us feeling warm inside, as if God were a cup of coffee . We ignore the fact that God is a king, that he is an angry God, a vengeful God, and a wrathful God. He is the judge and the priest. He is not playing games.

Peter goes on to say:

> If you address as Father the One who impartially judges according to each one's work, conduct yourselves in fear during the time of your stay on earth; knowing that you were not redeemed with perishable things like silver or gold from your futile way of life inherited from your forefathers, but with precious blood, as of a lamb unblemished and spotless, the blood of Christ.
>
> 1 Peter 1:17–19

All of these things are true, and all of them are equally important to us as Christians. God does have an infinite love for us, but with that comes discipline. God, being wholly good, is consumed by the supreme sense of justice in the universe, and he intends to see it carried out.

My goal for the rest of this book is to expel the shadows in our minds about some common vices in the Christian life, to remove our imposed grey and reveal the clear black and white beneath.

Hello? Is Anybody Listening?

Sex Outside of Marriage

> Marriage is to be held in honor among all, and the marriage bed is to be undefiled; for fornicators and adulterers God will judge.
>
> Hebrews 13:4

How exactly can I follow that up? Did you read the above verse? Need I say more? In today's world, sex isn't a big deal. To us, it simply doesn't matter. Watch any music video, listen to any song, and you'll hear all about said singer's "private time" with the special girl he just met like six minutes ago. And if a couple has been dating for over a year, the assumption is that they have had sex at least once. I mean it's been a whole year. If they haven't, either she's prude or he's secretly gay (but don't tell). It means that they truly love each other, right? Tell that to the man who spends his nights on business trips with prostitutes. I wonder, do you think he says he loves her? My guess is that he almost hates her as much as he hates himself for what he's doing. As a society, we have embraced our carnal pleasures and decided that fulfilling them however we want is acceptable.

Here's where we hit a roadblock. The Bible clearly disagrees (see verse above again if necessary, and again and again if still necessary). You see, there's this funny word in the above passage: *undefiled*. It means you show up to the honeymoon fresh-off-the-sex-boat, new and inexperienced. What am I saying? I'm saying: *virgin*. That's right. The Bible says that God wants sex to be saved for your spouse only. King Solomon says this:

> Let your fountain be blessed,
> And rejoice in the wife of your youth.
> As a loving hand and a graceful doe,
> Let her breasts satisfy you at all times;
> Be exhilarated always with her love.
> For why should you, my son, be exhilarated with an adulteress
> And embrace the bosom of a foreigner?

For the ways of a man are before the eyes of the
LORD,
And he watches all his paths.
His own iniquities will capture the wicked,
And he will be held with the cords of his sin.
He will die for lack of instruction,
And in the greatness of his folly he will go astray.

Proverbs 5:18–23

The passage above is admittedly initially humor-
ous for its rather unexpected imagery, but it also contains some powerful statements and impressive logic.
It encourages sex with your wife. No, this passage is
not sexist, it is written in the context of a father to his
son. But it asks, "Why should you, my son, be exhila-
rated with an adulteress and embrace the bosom of a
foreigner?" It clearly points out the danger of sex when
your wife is not involved.

Solomon points out that God sees everything a man
does, that the Lord "watches all his paths." From there,
he goes on to explain that sexual intercourse outside of
marriage is an "iniquity" and that the web he oblivi-
ously crafts from his own deeds will capture a man. If
his son pursues a sinful life, he will bring about his own
destruction. So, assuming that the Bible is indeed true,
we assume that this is indeed a command from God.
There. Simple.

I know, you really want to hook up with your partner, and controlling your hormones, your desires, and your lusts is incredibly difficult; but these things don't cloud the fact that God says: *No sex outside of marriage.* Funny thing, when we disobey God, we get punished. It's not really complicated or grey. It's actually quite clear. The big problem is not that we don't know what to do. It's that we don't want to know what to do.

Sex Outside of Marriage (In Your Head)

> You have heard that it was said, "You shall not commit adultery"; but I say to you that everyone who looks at a woman with lust for her has already committed adultery with her in his heart. If your right eye makes you stumble, tear it out and throw it from you; for it is better for you to lose one of the parts of your body, than for your whole body to be thrown into hell. If your right hand makes you stumble, cut it off and throw it from you; for it is better for you to lose one of the parts of your body, than for your body to go into hell.
>
> Matthew 5:27–30

I am extremely tempted to just write "End of Story" and dot it with a period. If you think about sex outside of marriage, you have just, for all intents and purposes, had sex outside of marriage. In case you missed the section actually about sex outside of marriage, look again. The Bible is clear that sex minus your wife, future or current, is wrong and brings about God's judgment.

The Bible is also clear that lust is equal to pre-marital, or extra-marital, sex in God's eyes and equally punishable. Speaking of which, if anyone actually applied the above policies literally, one could make a killing in the guide dog/guidance canes industry. Virtually every guy on earth would be blind, castrated, and missing at least one limb. Girls, I'm not exactly sure what you would be missing (haven't been in those shoes), but my guess is you would be missing something as well. Incidentally, I'm inclined to think the dramatic examples above are used to increase the effect of the point as to how dangerous lust is.

So, as to the famous question: how far is too far in a relationship? Well, I can't pretend to have an exact answer, but the guideline is clear. *No lust!* If some kind of "extracurricular activity" incites lust, it is not to be done because you have then fallen into sin. I'm not going to use one of the classic "don't do anything I wouldn't do" or "leave room for Jesus" sayings, but I think the boundary is clear in itself. There's no magic number of kisses (or minutes of kissing depending on if you ever breathe) that suddenly makes you lustful. There's no special cure-all. You just have to be actively responsible to avoid lust, so if that means no kissing (or leeching) in your relationship, then that is what the

Creator has asked of you. And as for that animalistic tribal dance we call "freak dancing," I think we all know why we dance like we are in bed with clothes on: *it feels good*. It's not because we can "feel the rhythm" (of the music at least) or because we "just want to dance." If that was our reasoning, we could do the tango or something. No, never mind, that's too artsy for our gorilla clan we call a generation.

Another thing: causing someone to sin is a sin in itself. Paul cautions the Corinthians, "But take care that this liberty of yours does not somehow become a stumbling block to the weak" (1 Corinthians 8:9). So, causing someone to lust is itself a sin. This means that girls, you should avoid wearing provocative clothing with the intent of making guys notice your looks. Let's be clear. I am not saying that girls (and guys) should get up in the morning and deliberately try to look ugly. That would be ridiculous in a totally different way! But we all know the difference between getting dressed to look nice and getting dressed to be, umm, "desirable." And if you haven't stopped to think about it, start now! It doesn't really matter if you didn't realize or weren't thinking about it. A sin in ignorance is a sin nonetheless.

True, you may choose to dress as such because of the fashions or for confidence. I have two responses. First, is being in fashion worth it if it causes a brother (or sister) to sin? It is incredibly fashionable to drink and have sex, but you will never see me excusing these behaviors because of societal whims. We called that peer pressure in Sunday school. Honestly, though, if you feel the need, I suppose you can just explain to God what the fashions of the times were and why you had to dress as such. As to the "confidence" argument, why do the clothes you wear provide confidence? If it's for a physical, impure reason, then you should take a long, hard look at your wardrobe. If not, you're in the green! (Yup, my guess is most of us just got stuck at a red light ...)

Guys, this does not remove our blame for our sins, it just pulls us both into the fray. The point is this: lust is clearly a sin according to the Bible (which we once again assume is true via the Christ), and instigating lust is as well. Don't do either. Confused? Probably not. Looking for reasons to be confused and say that: (a) you don't quite get it, or (b) can't help it, my eyes just look? My guess is yes. Yet again, if we really look at motives and the facts, we find a simple, clear-cut rule that we try to fuzzy because of what we want.

Potty-Mouth Syndrome

> And there must be no filthiness and silly talk, or coarse jesting, which are not fitting but rather giving of thanks. For this you know with certainty,

that no immoral or impure person or covetous man, who is an idolater, has an inheritance in the kingdom of Christ and God.

Ephesians 5:4–5

Now if we put the bits into the horses' mouths so that they will obey us, we direct their entire body as well. Look at the ships also, though they are so great and are driven by strong winds, are still directed by a very small rudder wherever the inclination of the pilot desires. So also the tongue is a small part of the body, and yet it boasts of great things. See how great a forest is set aflame by such a small fire. And the tongue is a fire, the very world of iniquity; the tongue is set among our members as that which defiles the entire body, and sets on fire the course of our life, and is set on fire by hell. For every species of beast and birds, of reptiles and creatures of the sea, is tamed and has been tamed by the human race. But no one can tame the tongue; it is a restless evil and full of deadly poison. With it we bless our LORD and Father, and with it we curse men, who have been made in the likeness of God; from the same mouth come both blessing and curse. My brethren, these things ought not to be this way.

James 3:3–10

First, I apologize for basically recording an entire book on swearing for you to read. In my defense, when I read the above passages, I thought they were both critical. The James section, especially, is an example of incredible writing and is filled with convicting power. Both contain a pretty clear command: control your words. Do not let any foul language or inappropriate talk come out of those two lips God has given you. I could be crazy, but the above passages seem like God's ideal punishment for swearing is going to be a lot worse than the classic "I'll wash your mouth out with soap" cinematic moment (cough, cough, death and eternal suffering, cough).

It often is debated what constitutes swearing. I was thinking about this, and I had this novel idea. If the world thinks that a word is "vulgar" in any degree, it probably is not a good thing to say. I know, crazy, right? Seriously though, I don't know how many times I have to hear the "I didn't know such-and-such was a bad word" argument before I intend to jump off a bridge (into a very deep, slow moving river eight feet below, of course). Come on people! Do I need a bullhorn here? *Look in the dictionary.* If it says in those neat little things called italics, "vulgar" it probably is not acceptable. The logic works like this. If Hitler were to, during World War II, see some murder occur and pause uncomfortably, suggesting that maybe they were going too far, then it was *definitely too far*. Get it? But this goes even beyond that, doesn't it? Paul suggests that there is to be "no coarse jesting" or any "filthiness" at all. Sex jokes are funny. I get it. But we have to see them for what they really are: inappropriate and wrong. The Bible is clear. None of that can come out of our mouths, and if laughing causes someone to keep telling them (which it does since no one keeps up with joking if no one laughs), then that also qualifies as causing someone to sin, which means no laughing either. Sorry. Try this on for size: if you wouldn't say this in front of your Grandma, then don't say it (unless of course you have some crazy grandma, then imagine a quiet, kitty-loving grandma and use that as your gauge).

Gossiping

> You shall not bear a false report; do not join your hand with a wicked man to be a malicious witness.
>
> Exodus 23:1

> For we hear that some among you are leading an undisciplined life, doing no work at all but acting like busybodies. Now such persons we command and exhort in the LORD Jesus Christ to work in quiet fashion and eat their own bread.
>
> 2 Thessalonians 3:11–12

> Like a club and a sword and a sharp arrow is a
> man who bears false witness against his neighbor.
>
> Proverbs 25:18

"Oh … my … gosh … Did you hear that Moses said that we shouldn't gossip or cheat or steal or tell lies? What a creeper!" I know. It sounds more than ridiculous when a person gossips about things like this. Why? Because it isn't some hushed-up rumor. It's not destructive. Why does this sound funny? Because people don't whisper when the thing being said is inoffensive and good-natured (unless it's a surprise, but my point still remains). Gossip is essentially when people say bad things that may or may not be true to each other minus the presence of the person involved. Gossip is by nature malicious. It wouldn't be worth it or fun if it was something everyone could hear and be happy about. Call me crazy, but this seems like one of those things that falls under the not-so-Christ-like category. The whole "love your neighbor as yourself" and "do unto others as you would have them do unto you" (or as beloved C.S. Lewis says, "Do as you would be done by") command is lost on gossip simply by its very nature. That's notwithstanding the three very clear scriptures above that condemn it as a dangerous, destructive, and sinful habit.

I love what Paul says in 2 Thessalonians. He basically says, "I heard some of you are talking trash about each other to pretend you are important. How about this: 'Get a job and do something with yourselves so that you actually are important.'" How often do we need to hear this when we waste hours on the phone talking about other people (O.M.G.! Did you hear that so-and-so hooked up with so-and-so?) Paul delivers the classic "Get a life." The last verse is basically a "sit down and shut up" of the Bible. Now, I understand that gossip is a cornerstone of people's social lives. You may be thinking that the earth is going to stand still and the sun will freeze over if you can't continue gossiping. I mean, you *have to* keep up on the latest news. My guess is that if you say this to God, that conversation from earlier with the man in court will happen to you. You will be greeted with a resounding, "*I don't care.*" Your social life and fantasies of popularity mean nothing in light of whether or not something is wrong and the fact that you will be punished for it.

Remember that thief who argued that he really wanted the thing he stole? Let's grow up and try not to be that person. We like to deal with absolutes when it comes to us being wronged, but we don't bind ourselves to the same rules. Even if we think our situation merits our release from these standards, it doesn't. Sorry. Good-bye gossip columns. Good-bye long phone calls about the latest drama. There's a choice here, even if we ignore it. If you gossip, you will suffer the consequences—no ifs, ands, ors, or buts. Game over. Either you believe Jesus, you don't believe him, or you don't care. I guess the decision is yours, but the only right choice seems pretty obvious to me.

Unequally Yoked

> Do not be bound together with unbelievers; for what partnership have righteousness and lawlessness, or what fellowship has light with darkness? Or what harmony has Christ with Belial, or what has a believer in common with an unbeliever. Or what agreement has the temple of God with idols? For we are the temple of the living God; just as God said, "I will dwell in them and walk among them; and I will be their God, and they shall be my people. Therefore, come out from their midst and be separate," says the LORD. "And do not touch what is unclean; and I will welcome you. And I will be a father to you, And you shall be sons and daughters to me," says the LORD Almighty,
>
> 2 Corinthians 6:14–18

The Bible sets out some pretty clear guidelines for relationships. If you are confused at this point, re-read the "do not be bound together with unbelievers" part again and again. I can't really say it any clearer than that. Here's another way of saying it: no close relationships with nonbelievers.

Why? First, the Bible said so. That should be enough. Secondly, two things of entirely different natures don't go together. Oil and water separate naturally, and they should! If they bound together closely, they wouldn't be oil and water anymore. Is that what we want (let alone what God wants) in our Christian lives? One or the other eventually has to give, and generally the corrupted doesn't become clean to accommodate the pure. No, it's usually the other way around. In other versions of this passage, it uses the term "unequally yoked" to evoke the idea of two oxen pulling a plow. You would never hook a big ox and a little ox to a plow. It would prevent them from going straight and would make things more difficult for the big oxen. Farmers, for best results, match up oxen of similar size.

Does this apply to dating? Yes! This is determinable through simple logic. In a relationship, you are looking for something. If it is anything other than comfort, emotional connection, possible marriage, or fellowship, it's probably sinful in nature (if "confused" about what I mean, see the above "Sex Outside of Marriage" section). Assuming, therefore, that these relationships exist for this deeply personal connection, then it is obvious that the above verse applies here as well. The point is simple: do not risk contaminating something that is clean.

Of course, people argue that it's "just dating"—to which I would suggest they should check their premises as to the nature of dating—or that they really like the person. Liking a person is a powerful feeling that dictates your thoughts almost entirely. In fact, it's consuming, like a wildfire. And really, who hasn't been there? Many times people argue that these feelings make it hard to resist, hard to control. Often people pull the "it's complicated" card (not the first time this theme has come up). But here's the thing: it's not complicated. It's *inconvenient*. There is a huge, fundamental difference that we cannot, as believers, ignore. The Bible is clear about its standards: none of this nonbeliever stuff. We just want to think it's complicated because it gives us an excuse to date the person we like, even if God doesn't approve. This *fact* is not undermined simply because you are already in a relationship with a nonbeliever. Now, if you are married to a nonbeliever, Paul has some different advice. You can look at 1 Corinthians 7 for his comments on that topic (since divorce is also generally forbidden by scripture).

For very similar reasons, this same passage and logic of two oxen work just as well in regard to friendships. Proverbs 27:17 says, "Iron sharpens iron, so one man sharpens another." By the same logic as used above, Christians should control who their friends (meaning more than just "hang out buddies") are and with whom they spend their time. The people around you influence

people can influence you
— close friends
girl friends

who you are. They have the power to either encourage or damage your faith and your ability to live an active Christian life.

As Christians, we are called to "abstain from our fleshly lusts" and remain out of the enemy's camp. Over and over again, the Bible hammers out the idea that you cannot straddle the fence in Christianity. A desire to avoid things of the world is encouraged and natural. David expresses a similar sentiment in Psalm 26 verses 4 and 5 saying, "I do not sit with deceitful men, nor will I go with pretenders. I hate the assembly of evildoers, and I will not sit with the wicked."

I need to pause and briefly clarify some of my statements. I am not saying that it is bad to associate with nonbelievers. We are called to do so! Jesus himself went and dined with the worst of the worst. He bathed with the refuse off the streets and the scum of man. But he didn't bring them in to make them his closest confidants. This passage in 2 Corinthians deals explicitly with any connections that are spiritually detrimental to the Christian testimony.

Part of the issue Paul was addressing was the Nicolaitan heresy, which had begun with compromises that allowed Christians to partake in pagan social and religious activities without guilt. Essentially, Paul reminded the church at Corinth that they were not allowed to partake in any spiritual venture with non-Christians. But that explanation does not in any way excuse keeping immoral company, as Paul states in 1 Corinthians 15:33 that bad company corrupts good morals (not to mention David's statements about company in Psalm 26).

Ultimately, as a Christian, there will always be a unique level of bonding that you can only achieve with a fellow Christian. Attempting to do so with a non-Christian is only detrimental to you. Being a friend involves an equally strong (in a different way) emotional and mental connection that has a certain degree of power in your life. The Bible calls for wisdom in relationships. In our closest, most intimate ones, we are ordered to make them fellow believers, men/women of similar mindset, whether they are friends, a "better" friend, or a spouse.

Drugs/Alcohol

> Submit yourselves for the LORD's sake to every human institution, whether to a king as the one in authority, or to governors as sent by him for the punishment of evildoers and the praise of those who do right. For such is the will of God that by doing right you may silence the ignorance of foolish men.
>
> 1 Peter 2:13–15

As obedient children, do not be conformed to the former lusts which were yours in your ignorance, but like the Holy One who called you, be holy yourselves also in all your behavior because it is written, "You shall be holy, for I am holy."

1 Peter 1:14–16

For the time already past is sufficient for you to have carried out the desire of the Gentiles, having pursued a course of sensuality, lusts, drunkenness, carousing, drinking parties and abominable idolatries.

1 Peter 4:3

And do not get drunk with wine, for that is dissipation, but be filled with the Spirit, speaking to one another in psalms and hymns and spiritual songs, singing and making melody with your heart to the LORD; always giving thanks for all things in the name of our LORD Jesus Christ to God, even the Father; and be subject to one another in the fear of Christ.

Ephesians 5:18–21

Flee immorality. Every other sin that a man commits is outside the body, but the immoral man sins against his own body. Or do you not know that your body is a temple of the Holy Spirit who is in you, whom you have from God, and that *you are not your own*?

you are not your own 1 Corinthians 6:18–19

"You are not your own." Wow. That is a powerful statement. Guess what? It's true. According to our assumptions, we believe that the statement that we are not our own is a true statement. How often have you stopped to think about that statement? Now, for this topic, I included a ton of scripture because I have a point to make. The Bible is very clear about the standards we should conduct ourselves by.

Today, it's normal for people to drink on a regular basis. The assumption is that you will drink or do drugs during your stay at the local high school. Most parents even accept this as a minor offense and just fatefully wait for the big confrontation. Kids think it's cool (grown-ups who think like this are really just hairy, wrinkly kids). They say it helps them relax and takes away the stress. It looks cool and people tend to get exactly what they are looking for (except that little dose of a drug that they never saw in the bottom of their drink).

Unfortunately for that crowd, the Bible lays down some clear boundaries for the consumption of intoxicating substances. It says two things. First, it says do not get drunk. Secondly, it says obey the law. These are very clear guidelines, and yet today we find people who seem to think it's okay for high school students to get drunk (Drunk equals intoxicated so that your behavior is impaired.). Guess what, it's not. It is a sin to disobey the law so that statement in itself means if you are younger than twenty-one, you can't drink. Sorry. And if you are older than twenty-one, you can't get drunk. My guess is that these guidelines are clear enough that you can figure out where you fit in this picture.

Now, it's easy to understand the allure that drinking parties hold. It is clearly fun, and it does temporarily help you forget your problems (and a lot of common sense too), but if you say these things to a judge with a keen sense of righteousness, my inclination is to think that he won't really sympathize with you all that much. Again, it's pretty black and white what is acceptable in a Christian's walk. We just like to think that it's hard to discern because it's convenient and gives us an excuse.

As for our need to experience life to relate, is this really the case? Do we need to experience something to know that it is wrong and that we will suffer the consequences? Not if we accept the Bible as absolute truth. The question is: do we? (Oh, and it is also advisable to avoid large amounts of alcohol because unlike other cells in your body, you can only experience the destruction of your liver cells once; they don't grow back. Just saying.)

" ... It's the Law"

> Submit yourselves for the LORD's sake to every
> human institution, whether to a king as the one
> in authority, or to governors as sent by him for the
> punishment of evildoers and the praise of those
> who do right. For such is the will of God that
> by doing right you may silence the ignorance of
> foolish men.
>
> 1 Peter 2:13–15

I included this verse again because this entails more
than just drugs and alcohol. A vast assortment of other
issues fit under the blanket of the law and respecting
authority. Of course, it's God's law to which we are
ultimately bound, so a law that violates God's law is to
be treated as sin.

Today, there's this huge trend towards "artistic
expression" and property damage. I say them as two
things, but really they can be one and the same. Graffiti
and such are sinful because they violate the law. The law
is heavily influenced by Christian morality. Regardless
of what people scream and shout, Christian men forged
the foundations of western society as we know it. Even
if the Bible did not clearly label stealing as wrong, it
would be simply because the government said it was.

The book of 1 Peter was written to a group of people
who were deeply suffering under the rule of Nero. They

were being subjected to a whole spectrum of persecution, including discrimination, having property confiscated, and death, all because they had the courage to tell a hostile world they were Christian. Naturally, they were unhappy in this society. All kinds of questions were coming up, including those of whether or not to obey Roman law. The last verse from above says, "For such is the will of God that by doing right you may silence the ignorance of foolish men" (1 Peter 2:15). He basically says Christians are called to obey the law so that they can be accused of no wrong. Here's the point: do not give the people you are trying to save a reason to believe that Christianity is no different from anything else. How many times do we have to share the gospel with people only to have them tell you that you're nothing special? The Creator calls us to be special because by our lives we can witness to the world. Jesus says this in the book of Matthew:

> You are the light of the world. A city set on a hill cannot be hidden; nor does anyone light a lamp and put it under a basket, but on the lampstand, and it gives light to all who are in the house. Let your light shine before men in such a way that they may see your good works, and glorify your Father who is in heaven.
>
> Matthew 5:14–16

As Christians, we are called to witness through our lives. The Bible is clear that we are to submit to authority and the government in order to make this possible. There is no vagueness here. *Submit to auth & govt*

America's Idols

> Therefore, since we have so great a cloud of witnesses surrounding us, let us also lay aside every encumbrance and the sin which so easily entangles us, and let us run with endurance the race that is set before us, fixing our eyes on Jesus, the author and perfecter of faith, who for the joy set before him endured the cross, despising the shame, and has sat down at the right hand of the throne of God.
>
> Hebrews 12:1–2

Ah, idolatry. It's a strange topic at first glance, really. People don't really worship idols today, do they? ("No Mom, I have to pray to my golden calf first!") It's really bizarre then that the Bible would spend so much time emphasizing *no idols*, especially considering it is a book of absolute truth that is absolutely relevant, right? I think deep down we all know what it means in today's world when we say that we cannot have any idols before God. Okay, maybe it's really deep down there.

In the passage from Hebrews above, it tells us to fix our eyes on Jesus. That means complete focus on him, on "the author and perfecter of faith." This makes logical sense. We should focus on him who saved us from our own depravity and gave us an eternal gift, right?

So since the goal is total focus on God, here's my proposal: anything that takes away a part of our focus from God is now officially an idol. Anything at all. Maybe you're skipping out on youth group to hang out with your girlfriend, or maybe you can't tithe because of your drug addiction (granted, tithing has to be from the heart anyways). Perhaps you "can't" have a private Bible study because you have football every day. Maybe as a father, hosting a family prayer time doesn't fit in your schedule because you are struggling in this poor economy. Anything can be good, and anything can be done in worship. Where it becomes bad is when the focus is no longer on God but on the thing, and time with this thing is now the priority of your life.

Let's picture a Major League Baseball player. He's an immensely talented player and just got drafted. He has a lot of potential to be successful. Now he's also known for an intense World of Warcraft obsession (as in, he would let his dog starve if he was in the middle of something big). Now of course this major sports opportunity is a much wiser and profitable course for him to take, and you would expect him to dedicate himself entirely to growing in his skill as a baseball player and improving with his team. But let's say he skips practice regularly to play his videogame. His skill slips, and he eventually falls far behind his teammates until he reaches the point that his coach kicks him off the team. What an opportunity wasted! How dumb would you say this person was? He forfeited millions of dollars for a game, for a temporary distraction.

Why is it we live our Christian lives like this? Maybe you have some "World of Warcraft" in your life that is keeping you from focusing on the one thing that really matters in this world—the eternal message of redemption provided by Jesus Christ. This thing (or things) is an idol, and the Bible is more than clear; it has to go. If it distracts from your vision and focus on the author and perfecter of our faith, it is a tool to distract, whether it's videogames, friends, a girlfriend/boyfriend, a job, or even food. Once that threshold is crossed—and if we are honest, it's not that hard to determine if it has been—it has become an idol and has to be dealt with accordingly.

Lying (and Yes, White Ones Count Too)

> But above all, my brethren, do not swear, either by heaven or by earth or with any other oath; but your yes is to be yes, and your no, no, so that you may not fall under judgment.
>
> James 5:12

Again, you have heard that the ancients were told, "You shall not make false vows, but shall fulfill your vows to the LORD." But I say to you, make no oath at all, either by heaven, for it is the throne of God, or by the earth, for it is the footstool of his feet, or by Jerusalem, for it is the city of the great King. Nor shall you make an oath by your head, for you cannot make one hair white or black. But let your statement be, "Yes, yes" or "No, no"; anything beyond these is of evil.

Matthew 5:33–37

You shall not bear false witness against your neighbor.

Exodus 20:16

"If only you had told me the truth. I was more mad that you lied." How many times have we all heard that? It seems to be a sort of broken record that we all have programmed inside us and have to listen to outside of us. It's funny really; we all hate to be lied to, and yet we all lie. But is lying really the issue? Here's the thing: we all define it as telling someone something that is not true. But that hardly even scratches the surface of the biblical standard for a Christian's words, and presumably, that is the definition we care about. Anything that is absent of truth and reality is a sin. So, if you "stretch the truth" or leave out a little detail that changes the

anything absent of truth/reality is a sin.

overall perception ("I didn't know they would see it that way…" wink, wink) is a lie.

But it's even bigger than that. It's about *commitment* to what you say. You are called as a Christian to mean what you say, nothing more, nothing less. If you say you will do something, do it. If you say you won't do something, don't. The implications of this for relationships, work, service, ministry, and parenting are endless, but I'll leave the personal introspection to you. You shouldn't have to sign anything or initiate a pact in blood in order for your promises and claims to be taken as legitimate. What does that imply about your word's value if you have to sell your soul to the devil to prove it? When someone asks you something, tell him or her "the truth, the whole truth, and nothing but the truth so help me God" (ironic because it comes from an oath you make in court). Nowadays, we have commitment issues, obviously. If you want to clear a room of high school students without a bomb threat or money, ask them to commit to something involving responsibilities. But the Bible tells us to commit to our words, to invest ourselves in them. If we can do that, everything will change. This also includes cheating. How? Well, you turn your work in with your name on it, and the implication is that you did it. Granted, you don't literally say you did, but the implication behind you claiming credit is that you are responsible for the work. The absence of you saying otherwise is an absence of truth.

meaning it's wrong. Marriage fits under this as well. Your oath on the wedding day is an oath. It doesn't change because you no longer like the perfume/cologne your spouse wears. As Christians, we are called to the truth because Christ is truth. Let's start acting like it.

Homosexuality

> For this reason God gave them over to degrading passions; for their women exchanged the natural function for that which is unnatural, and in the same way also the men abandoned the natural function of the woman and burned in their desire toward one another, men with men committing indecent acts and receiving in their own persons the due penalty of their error.
>
> Romans 1:26–27

> You shall not lie with a male as one lies with a female; it is an abomination.
>
> Leviticus 18:22

> But we know that the Law is good, if one uses it lawfully, realizing the fact that law is not made for a righteous person, but for those who are lawless and rebellious, for the ungodly and sinners, for the unholy and profane, for those who kill their fathers or mothers, for murderers and immoral

men and homosexuals and kidnappers and liars and perjurers, and whatever else is contrary to sound teaching, according to the glorious gospel of the blessed God, with which I have been entrusted.

1 Timothy 1:8–11

This is one of those sensitive subjects that people try to avoid, because with this, as with personal relationships, it involves a vast amount of internal emotions and feelings that we see as making things "complicated." In our world today, homosexuality has become acceptable and protected. Someone who "comes out" is often seen as courageous. People who speak out against homosexuality are often labeled as "homophobic" or hateful, often akin to racism. Granted, people often speak out in hate, but the labels are also applied to those who don't. And as a church, we have allowed society's tolerance to infiltrate the church. Some churches even argue that it is not actually wrong. If that's the case, then I must need to work on my reading comprehension skills or something because it would seem that I am failing at reading the above passages and understanding what is being said. Honestly, I'm inclined to think (or at least hope) otherwise. We have turned the issue grey to suit our needs.

I understand that there are a ton of emotional considerations and that one may have these desires, but that does not change the fact that the Bible is clear. Homosexuality is a sin. Bottom line. There really isn't room for debate. The debate about whether these desires are natural or if one is born with them is interesting but irrelevant to the big picture. The Bible calls for you to turn away from your desires in plenty of other cases aside from homosexuality, including heterosexual sex outside of marriage.

Christians do have to be careful, though, because as is often said, "Hate the sin, not the sinner." The passage from 1 Timothy above appeals to that mentality. The gospel was not meant for perfect people, it exists to aid those who are in sin (which, funny enough, is all of us). Homosexuality is a sin, but like all sins, it can be forgiven. Therefore, Christians are called, in fact demanded, to condemn the act but also to work in love to help the one in sin to heal and be reconciled to Christ.

John says this, "If we confess our sins, he is faithful and righteous to forgive us our sins and to cleanse us from all unrighteousness" (1 John 1:9). Our perspective as Christians cannot change. God's law is eternal and does not bend to fit our temporal whims. Homosexuality is a sin, and thus must be viewed accordingly.

Gambling

Make sure that your character is free from the love of money, being content with what you have; for he Himself has said, "I will never leave you nor will I ever forsake you."

Hebrews 13:5

But those who want to get rich fall into temptation and a snare and many foolish and harmful desires which plunge men into ruin and destruction. For the love of money is a root of all sorts of evil, and some by longing for it have wandered away from the faith and pierced themselves with many griefs.

1 Timothy 6:9–10

For you yourselves know how you ought to follow our example, because we did not act in an undisciplined manner among you, nor did we eat anyone's bread without paying for it, but with labor and hardship we kept working night and day so that we would not be a burden to any of you; not because we do not have the right to this, but in order to offer ourselves as a model for you, so that you would follow our example.

2 Thessalonians 3:7–9

Gambling is one of those tricky issues because none of the "key words" are used. The Bible doesn't explicitly say, "Gambling is bad," like it does for other issues such as drunkenness or homosexuality. Thus, a lot of people like to claim the "Christian freedom" tagline when it comes to gambling. Basically, it is argued that since it is not explicitly mentioned, it's not exactly a bad thing and is acceptable for a Christian in moderation. But I would argue that gambling is *thematically* bad. Does that make sense? It's kind of like this: Shooting someone in the leg is not explicitly stated as bad since they are not murdered when you do so, but it is obviously wrong. Why? Because it is lacking in several key Christian qualities such as, oh, I don't know, love, self control, gentleness, and a whole slew of others. Granted, it's also illegal, but I digress.

The big question we have to ask is: Why do people gamble? They gamble to get lucky and win money the easy way. Now you may argue that it is for the fun of competition and that it is simply exciting, but then that of course leads you to the question of why it is exciting, which leads us back again to money. Judging from the verses above, does this sound like a healthy practice? The Bible is clear that we must avoid the love of money at all costs for this desire brings with it "all sorts of evil" (not *all* evil as is so often misquoted thanks to less specific translations). The passage from 2 Thessalonians makes the point that although Paul had the right to "mooch" off of other people's money, it was not suitable to a person of Christian character. He points out that it's not explicitly wrong, but rather that it is inappropriate for a Christian to be a burden to another.

Of course, there's the whole common sense factor where you should see the huge casino palace where you are trying to win money and think, "Gee, I wonder where they get all their money?" I mean, really? Is this the responsible choice? "I don't have enough money so I am going to go risk it at a casino where I am obviously likely to lose so they can pay the bills." Ummm ... all right. If this sounds okay, then hopefully moral persuasion can convince you otherwise.

You may be able to gamble without any "love for money" or desire to earn your money the easy way (is earning it via gambling ever "the hard way"?), but when you take away the motivator, would that really be fun?

Divorce

> Some Pharisees came up to Jesus, testing him, and began to question him whether it was lawful for a man to divorce a wife. And he answered them and said to them, "What did Moses command you?" They said, "Moses permitted a man to write a certificate of divorce and send her away." But Jesus said to them, "Because of your hardness of heart

he wrote you this commandment. But from the beginning of creation, God made them male and female. For this reason a man shall leave his father and mother and the two shall become one flesh; so they are no longer two, but one flesh. What therefore God has joined together, let no man separate." In the house the disciples began questioning him about this again. And he said to them, "Whoever divorces his wife and marries another woman commits adultery against her; and if she herself divorces her husband and marries another man, she is committing adultery."

Mark 10:2–12

In today's day and age, divorce is more common than staying married. It just seems natural that if you "stop loving" your spouse you should leave them. Unfortunately, the Bible is clearly dead-set against this idea. Here, Jesus points out that Moses allowed divorce because we as people couldn't stick to our commitments, but that didn't mean it was okay. He references Genesis 2 as well, quoting the "become one flesh" passage. The idea is that marriage unites two separate people into one under God's holy blessing, and no man should ever tear it apart. If you decided you didn't like your toes, would you tear off the lower half of your body? No! And neither should we as Christians tear apart a body over human scruples. God intended marriage to be permanent. We as fallible creatures don't really sit well with that idea, so we twist it to make up our own reality that suits us. We argue all of the emotional damage and harm being done, but even here, we defeat ourselves by using selfish arguments in defense of an act proclaimed as wrong. Again, our hearts as sinful creatures get in the way and defeat us, focusing our care on self-interest and creating a rift that is dangerous to us as believers.

Aside from the direct command, it is also a simple violation of our word, which the Bible also clearly prohibits. In the section on lying, the following verse appears:

> But above all, my brethren, do not swear, either by heaven or by earth or with any other oath; but your yes is to be yes, and your no, no, so that you may not fall under judgment.
>
> James 5:12

Divorce breaks a covenant one makes with their spouse, violating a promise. Hebrews 9:17 tells us that a "covenant is valid only when men are dead, for it is never in force while the one who made it lives." This is true in a marriage covenant. If broken off before death, then the covenant was violated and an additional sin has entered the arena. Regardless of our fickle emotions, the Bible is clear. No divorce. If divorce does happen, it also provides very strict regulations for the individual's conduct. Let us be people of our word and of truth. Maybe then Christians will stop reporting nearly identical marital statistics as the rest of the world and start being that city on a hill. After all, who are we to be so arrogant as to separate what "God has joined together"?

The Pack 10   *10 Comm.!*

And God spoke all these words:

"I am the LORD your God, who brought you out of Egypt, out of the land of slavery.

"You shall have no other gods before me.

"You shall not make for yourself an idol in the form of anything in heaven above or on the earth beneath or in the waters below. You shall not bow down to them or worship them; for I, the LORD your God, am a jealous God, punishing the children for the sin of the fathers to the third and fourth generation of those who hate me, but showing love to a thousand generations of those who love me and keep my commandments.

"You shall not misuse the name of the LORD your God, for the LORD will not hold anyone guiltless who misuses his name.

"Remember the Sabbath day by keeping it holy. Six days you shall labor and do all your work, but the seventh day is a Sabbath to the LORD your God. On it you shall not do any work, neither you, nor your son or daughter, nor your manservant or maidservant, nor your animals, nor the alien within your gates. For in six days the LORD made the heavens and the earth, the sea, and all that is in them, but he rested on the seventh day. Therefore the LORD blessed the Sabbath day and made it holy.

"Honor your father and your mother, so that you may live long in the land the LORD your God is giving you.

"You shall not murder.

"You shall not commit adultery.

"You shall not steal.

"You shall not give false testimony against your neighbor.

"You shall not covet your neighbor's house. You shall not covet your neighbor's wife, or his manservant or maidservant, his ox or donkey, or anything that belongs to your neighbor."

Exodus 20:1–17 (NIV)

Umm ... yeah ... Any questions? No? Okay, good.

*Note: the first ones deal with your relationship with God. The rest of them deal with your relationship with man. Priorities, maybe?

The Contemplative Lifestyle

Then the LORD spoke to Moses, "Go down at once, for your people, whom you brought up from the land of Egypt have corrupted themselves. They have quickly turned aside from the way which I commanded them. They have made for themselves a molten calf, and have worshiped it and have sacrificed to it and said, 'This is your god, O Israel, who brought you up from the land of Egypt.'" The LORD said to Moses, "I have seen this people and behold, they are an obstinate people. Now then let Me alone, that My anger may burn against them and that I may destroy them; and I will make of you a great nation."

Exodus 32:7–10

Jesus said to him, "I am the way, and the truth, and the life; no one comes to the Father but through Me. If you had known Me, you would have known my Father also; from now on you know him, and have seen him." Phillip said to him, "LORD, show us the Father, and it is enough for us." Jesus said to him, "Have I been so long with you, and yet you have not come to know Me, Phillip? He who has seen Me has seen the Father; how can you say, 'Show us the father?' Do you not believe that I am in the Father, and the Father is in Me? The words that I say to you I do not speak on My own initiative, but the Father abiding in Me does his works.

John 14:6–10

Submit therefore to God. Resist the devil and he will flee from you. Draw near to God and he will draw near to you. Cleanse your hands, you sinners; and purify your hearts you double-minded. Be miserable and mourn and weep; let your laughter be turned into mourning and your joy to gloom. Humble yourselves in the presence of the LORD, and he will exalt you.

James 4:7–10

For by grace you have been saved through faith; and that not of yourselves, it is the gift of God; not as a result of works, so that no one may boast.

Ephesians 2:8–9

See to it that no one takes you captive through philosophy and empty deception, according to *C 28* the tradition of men, according to the elementary principles of the world rather than according to Christ. For in him all the fullness of Deity dwells in bodily form, and in him you have been made complete, and he is the head over all rule and authority; and in him you were also circumcised with a circumcision made without hands, in the removal of the body of the flesh by the circumcision of Christ; having been buried with him in baptism, in which you were also raised up with him through faith in the working of God, who raised him from the dead.

Colossians 2:8–12

For if those who are of the Law are heirs, faith is made void and the promise is nullified; for the Law brings about wrath, but where there is no law, there also is no violation.

Romans 4:14–15

For even though they knew God, they did not honor him as God or give thanks, but they became futile in their speculations, and their foolish heart was darkened. Professing to be wise, they became fools, and exchanged the glory of the incorruptible God for an image in the form of corruptible man and of birds and four-footed animals and crawling creatures. Therefore God gave them over in the lusts of their hearts to impurity, so that their bodies would be dishonored among them. For they exchanged the truth of God for a lie, and worshiped and served the creature rather than the Creator, who is blessed forever. Amen.

Romans 1:21–25

Do not turn to mediums or spiritists; do not seek them out to be defiled by them. I am the LORD your God.

Leviticus 19:31

But the Spirit explicitly says that in later times some will fall away from the faith, paying attention to deceitful spirits and doctrines of demons.

1 Timothy 4:1

I know, I picked a boatload of verses. That's my point. You see, a common practice in today's church is called contemplative prayer. This practice has *no biblical basis*, whatsoever. None. Proponents argue that the verse "Be still and know that I am God" is the basis for such a practice, but in the more literal NASB translation it says, "Stop striving and know that I am God" (Psalm 46:10). Even more in favor of my point, in full context it clearly has no bearing whatsoever on any form of "spiritual discipline" involving a silencing of the mind. It says this:

Come, behold the works of the LORD,
Who has wrought desolations in the earth.
He makes wars to cease to the end of the earth;
He breaks the bow and cuts the spear in two;
He burns the chariots with fire.
Cease striving and know that I am God;

I will be exalted among the nations, I will be
exalted in the earth.

Psalm 46: 8–10

The full context of this passage makes it clear: this
has *nothing* to do with any form of unique prayer whatsoever. Rather, it is reminding a nation at war to trust
in the Lord who, in the end, will prevail. Proponents
have no other verses in favor of a biblical basis to this
practice.

Beyond the lack of biblical support, I would argue
that it is indeed *unbiblical* on several grounds. But
first, what exactly is said about contemplative prayer?
What is it? According to contemplativeprayer.net, the
process is a "contemplative meditation as a teachable,
spiritual process, enabling the ordinary person to enter
and receive a direct experience of union with God."
Oftentimes, it involves repeating a word or phrase continuously until one's mind is "empty" and one enters an
alternate state. Other times, it may involve a technique
using a prayer map called a *labyrinth* that is used to
"guide the mind" into the center.

First, this undermines a basic tenant of Christianity.
Why do we "ordinary" people need this method? The
Bible is clear in John 14 how one comes to know God.
Jesus himself says that he is "the way, and the truth,
and the life" and that "no one comes to the Father but

through [him]." He makes it clear. Jesus, as our Savior, is the path to God and nothing else can take that place. Phillip asks Jesus to show him the Father—in a sense, asks Christ for something more. And Jesus responds by questioning his faith. Why would we need something beyond Jesus if he truly does bring us into the presence of the Almighty God? Jesus is asking: Do we doubt his ability? Beyond that, what of the Holy Spirit? Do we not need him anymore? The Bible is clear that once you are saved, you are indwelled by the Holy Spirit and, thus, are in the presence of God. You do not need to do something special for him to be there. He just is. He never leaves only to come when you enter an "altered state." He has his room, and he is there to stay. He doesn't need you to come build him another one every day. After all, he is God, isn't he?

Secondly, it is based on the assumption that God is in everyone. This is simply false. The Bible is clear that God cannot fellowship with imperfection and that light has no place with darkness. Thus, unless one is saved, God is not "in" said individual. This also undermines salvation. If God were in everyone, and we could practice this little technique to reach him, then why was his Son butchered on a cross? It would be useless! Paul describes it like this:

> For if those who are of the Law are heirs, faith is made void and the promise is nullified; for the

Law brings about wrath, but where there is no law, there also is no violation.

Romans 4:14–15

His point is this: if someone could be saved through actions they could do, then salvation is nullified. If salvation is nullified, then guess what? So is Christianity! And if contemplative prayer is not meant to bring anyone to God and is simply for Christians, then it does what is unnecessary since, according to Jesus, we are already in the presence of God.

Colossians 2 warns us clearly to not get caught up in empty philosophy and deceive ourselves. It says that we have been exposed to the *fullness* of God in Christ and that through him we are made *whole*. Not half filled. Not partially finished. He says *whole*. There is nothing left to add beyond the absolute truth of *I Am* as presented through Jesus Christ. In salvation we have become new creatures who already posses the Holy Spirit in its entirety; we just need to listen and not look for an easy way to know truth. That is exactly what Adam and Eve did, and we all know how that turned out.

In Romans, it talks of those who have turned to human "wisdom" and, in doing so, embraced foolishness. We need to stop looking for supposed methods of old and turn to the eternal Word of the Almighty God for our instruction and inspiration. Proponents argue that it has been a part of Christianity for thousands of years. Fantastic. Slavery was a part of almost all of America's history. Shall we hold on to that too?

Additionally, some argue that they have received wisdom and insight from what some call their "Spirit Guide" while in this altered state of consciousness. I would hasten to point out that as Christians, as I have continuously repeated thus far, we believe that the Bible is perfect and eternal, and therefore full of wisdom. If it is perfect, why do we need additional wisdom imparted? God will fully reveal himself through his Word. Why must we actively pursue another source of wisdom? Also, how do we know that the voice imparting wisdom is indeed of God? Have we stopped to consider the real possibility that the voice could be less than benevolent in intent? Yes, demonic spirits can indeed tell us helpful information in order to sway us in the wrong direction.

In his book *The Christian in Complete Armour*, author William Gurnall discusses what he calls "spiritual adultery" saying, "We see this happening in the church today, where a faction embraces some doctrinal error or flaming heresy, and contends for it with more zeal than for the simple gospel truths that led them to Christ in the first place. The loss in such instances is great, for Christ can never share true, conjugal love with a soul that is coupling with error" (202). Isn't it amazing how a puritan, who has been dead for four hundred years, described with such clarity the danger we face today? Oh, and just as a minor detail: Jesus himself has instructed us how to pray, and it had nothing to do with anything described by proponents of the contemplative techniques.

*For more on contemplative spirituality, I highly recommend *A Time of Departing* by Ray Yungen.

Garbage in, Garbage ... Well, You Know

> But you did not learn Christ in this way, if indeed you have heard him and have been taught in him, just as truth is in Jesus, that, in reference to your former manner of life, you lay aside the old self, which is being corrupted in accordance with the lusts of deceit, and that you be renewed in the spirit of your mind, and put on the new self, which in the likeness of God has been created in righteousness and holiness of the truth.
>
> Ephesians 4:20–24

> But immorality or any impurity or greed must not even be named among you, as is proper among saints; and there must be no filthiness and silly talk or course jesting, which are not fitting, but rather giving of thanks.
>
> Ephesians 5:3–4

You have heard that it was said, "You shall not commit adultery"; but I say to you that everyone who looks at a woman with lust for her has already committed adultery with her in his heart.

Matthew 5:27–28

But take care that this liberty of yours does not somehow become a stumbling block to the weak.

1 Corinthians 8:9

So I have to admit, I titled this with vicious intent. See, most of you probably saw it, and probably smirked, chuckled, or maybe simply filled in the blank with a, "Yeah, we know." But here's the thing: Apparently, we don't. The Bible, as established in the "Potty-Mouth Syndrome" section, clearly states that we are to abstain from course humor and inappropriate jokes. We are to avoid lust with all seriousness because, as Jesus makes clear, it is a destructive wildfire. And we are to avoid making others sin. So frankly, what media we "consume" has more than just one reason to be censored.

My guess is that many of you like those "soft core" scenes in rated "R" movies a little more than you should. And I would also wager that most of us laugh when we shouldn't at those comedies and comedy routines that talk about sex, drugs, alcohol, unfaithfulness … you name it. We laugh. We shouldn't. And here's the more direct problem: _we go_. We have no place there. If you know an environment will incline you to sin (and yes, you can know based on common sense), we should not be there. And we know. It is really simple nowadays to look up a film's ratings online and get the reasoning behind the letter. The challenge is minimal when it comes to watching a *green band* movie trailer and discerning if the movie will be inappropriate.

As Christians, we are called to leave our old life behind us, to abandon our lifestyle of sin that we have so completely embraced in our past. We are called to come out of the darkness. And we say we have, but frankly, many of us still haven't entirely. I'm calling on you today to move into the light in its entirety. Partial surrender is not enough. You cannot serve two masters. It is time to choose.

Another thing to consider: we are told not to make others stumble. In a free market society, we as the consumers possess this thing called "consumer sovereignty." We vote for the products we want by spending our money. Your presence is partially responsible for the presence of these inappropriate films and, thus, partially responsible for the sin of those around us in the theater.

Beyond that, think of the influence you have on whether or not your friends attend. They may reconsider going if you refuse to attend. Of course, they could go alone, but that is a different story entirely. And it is not simply movies. It is magazines, the Internet, radio, music, comedians, and many more. Imagine if we as Christians all decided to censor what we watched and listened to. The industry would look entirely different.

Teeth Whitening and Jesus

So what exactly is the point of all this? Why did I set out to make a list of obvious sins and explain where it says they are wrong? Well, frankly, it's because apparently they aren't so obvious. Apparently, the car isn't the logical first place to check for your keys. Oh, wait. Never mind. It is. We as society are just collectively idiotic.

Here's the thing. These may seem obvious, but if that's the case (which I am arguing it is), why is it that we continue to mess it up anyway? The world in a moral perspective is black and white. God has made it very clear what he expects of us in our daily lives. We simply look for the "grey areas" to excuse ourselves for our sins. How much easier is it to sin if we are convinced it is a burden we cannot bear? Keep in mind, the Bible is clear that you will never face a sin you cannot overcome. Paul encourages his readers from the church at Corinth:

> No temptation has overtaken you but such as is common to man; and God is faithful, who will not allow you to be tempted beyond what you are able; but with the temptation will provide the way of escape also, so that you will be able to endure it.
>
> 1 Corinthians 10:13

You will never face a battle you cannot overcome. Yet the reality is that we probably, in some situations, will not. Why is that, exactly? I want to propose three reasons. First, we as humans are inclined toward our sin nature due to the fabulous original sin. This is where every wisecracking guy says, "Thanks, *Eve*." (No, I don't blame woman for man's problems.) And, if we look at all of God's laws throughout the Old Testament, specifically Leviticus, it can seem a tad staggering and impossible. That's the point. The writer of Hebrews explains:

> For the Law, since it has only a shadow of the
> good things to come and not the very form of
> things, can never, by the same sacrifices which
> they offer continually year by year, make perfect
> those who draw near. Otherwise, would they not
> have ceased to be offered, because the worshipers,
> having once been cleansed, would no longer have
> consciousness of sins? But in those sacrifices there
> is a reminder of sins year by year. For it is impos-
> sible for the blood of bulls and goats to take away
> sins.

Hebrews 10:1–4

The law of the Old Testament and the sacrifices
served as a continual reminder of the people's impurity,
so that the need for a messiah, a final anointed sacrifice, could be fully understood when the time came.
And what a beautiful message it is. God became man,
fully man and fully God, to die for our sins and make
us pure since we as people could never do so ourselves.
And in his blood, in his suffering, we are made pure. In
what I like to call "the gospel according to Isaiah," the
prophet says this:

> But he was pierced through for our transgressions,
> He was crushed for our iniquities;
> The chastening for our well-being fell upon him,
> And by his scourging we are healed.

All of us like sheep have gone astray,
Each of us has turned to his own way;
But the Lord has caused the iniquity of us all
To fall on him.

Isaiah 53:5–6

Wow. That is a message of eternal and transcendent power. The writer of Hebrews says this:

But when Christ appeared as a high priest of the good things to come, he entered through the greater and more perfect tabernacle, not made with hands, that is to say, not of this creation; and not through the blood of goats and calves, but through his own blood, he entered the holy place once for all, having obtained eternal redemption.

Hebrews 9:11–12

The reality is this: all mankind, due to their sinful nature and God's holy nature, are destined to die and suffer for all eternity in hell, separated from God and all good forever. But God, in his infinite love and mercy, provided an alternative to hell so that we could spend eternity with him, in the presence of eternal good instead. Some may call Christianity exclusive, but why would you refuse an offer for help simply because it's not presented in the way you imagined it should be? The reality of heaven, hell, and the depravity of our own hearts must always be understood. If we lose sight of where we have come from, then what inspiration is there to live up to our calling? What necessity bears salvation if we do not need saving? Original sin is prevalent in all of our failings, really, because what this boils down to is our *desire* to do such a thing.

I also believe another major contributor to our failure is the absence of a healthy, reverent fear of the Lord. I think society has reacted strongly against the fire and brimstone of a bygone era. We have this fear of turning people off of Christianity because apparently it's all about us. Instead, I think we have gone to the other extreme, one perhaps just as dangerous if not more. Is this why Christians are apathetic in their service? Have we forgotten who God is? The Bible emphasizes over and over and over again that we are to fear God.

You know, there's this crazy dude in the Old Testament, you may have heard of him. He was known by most (actually, all) as Solomon. He's famous because God asked him what he wanted, saying he would give him one thing, and Solomon asked for wisdom. God proceeded to grant this request, as well as give him a ton of money and power. (He was king for quite a while.) That guy, Solomon, the man who possessed wisdom from God said, "The fear of the Lord is the beginning of knowledge; Fools despise wisdom and instruction" (Proverbs 1:7). Did you catch that? Solomon said that the fear of the Lord was the *beginning*, as in square one.

If you don't get this, you do not know anything, so says the wisest man ever. There are multiple other places in Scripture that emphasize this idea. A few are included below:

> You shall fear only the LORD your God; and you shall worship him and swear by his name. You shall not follow other gods, any of the gods of the peoples who surround you, for the LORD your God in the midst of you is a jealous God; otherwise the anger of the LORD your God will be kindled against you, and he will wipe you off the face of earth.

> Deuteronomy 6:13–15

> He who sits in the heavens laughs,
> The LORD scoffs at them.
> Then he will speak to them in his anger
> And terrify them in his fury, saying,
> But as for Me, I have installed My King
> Upon Zion, My holy mountain.

> Psalm 2:4–6

> The conclusion, when all has been heard, is: fear God and keep his commandments, because this applies to every person. For God will bring every act to judgment, everything which is hidden, whether it is good or evil.

> Ecclesiastes 12:13–14

> So then, my beloved, just as you have always obeyed, not as in my presence only, but now much more in my absence, work out your salvation with fear and trembling; for it is God who is at work in you, both to will and to work for his good pleasure.

> Philippians 2:12–13

The Hebrew word for fear is *Yir'ah*, which is used in the Old Testament to describe fear, terror, or an object causing said emotions. The Greek word is *phobos* which is used to translate into a fear, dread, or terror. Isn't that indicative of what exactly it means when the Bible says, "Fear God"? Have you ever stopped and thought about the nature of that command? I think part of the problem is that most of us alive today, at least those of us in my generation and the majority of the world, have never lived under a monarch. We have democracy here in the enlightened West. Don't mistake me, I am a huge fan of democracy, but I also believe we have lost a certain sense of being totally underneath someone, in submission. We have lost that fear of the kings of old. This fear wasn't a hateful fear always, either. If you read literature of the time or about the time, there's always this sense of reverent awe for royalty. At least in her early years, people adored Catherine the Great, but they still would be shaking and their hands would be sweaty at the thought of speaking in front of her. And if she spoke, the entire nation jumped and strained to hear. It was a love, but a love that included recognition of station, something we have lost today entirely.

His laws and demands for our behavior are not to be treated as suggestions from our friends. He says, "No sexual impurity." That's it. That's all. He means none. None at all. He's not saying, "If you do it, I'll forgive you and everything will be okay." He's saying, "No, none at all, and if you do, you can talk to me and I will forgive you, but you will still have consequences." We love to think about forgiveness, but we ignore the consequences. There's a logical fallacy there. Forgiveness does not void the impact of our actions. Galatians 6:7 says, "Do not be deceived. God is not mocked; for whatever a man sows, this he will also reap." I often wonder what Christians would be like if they actually understood this.

Imagine being invited to the White House. Picture sitting there, and all of a sudden your little brother starts to destroy everything. Everything. What would you be thinking? *What an idiot. Oh my word! No! No! No! That's the president's desk! He's going to kill us.* Yeah, well, the president is powerful, in fact, arguably the most powerful, but Psalm 2 says God scoffs at the rulers of the world. How is it that we don't feel bad doing this to God's house? Would we sit and talk at church? Would we sit politely, listen, and let one word go in one ear and out the other? Would we party on Fridays or do stuff with our girlfriends on Saturdays? Would we argue with our parents and find humor in rebelling against our elders? Would we turn prayer into a joke? Would we look at porn or skip church because we're tired? Would we tell dirty jokes? Would we treat people like dirt if we understood that they were God's possessions? What would it be like if we understood God's Word as what it actually is? Not as suggestions, but as commands. Do you think about the fact that the almighty Creator of the universe is watching you at every moment—when you are sitting here, when you are with your girlfriend, when you are at that New Year's party? The God of the Old Testament and of the New Testament is the same God as he is today. Do you believe that? Do you? Honestly?

When someone speaks from the Word, do you remember in two weeks? I had the opportunity to speak at a winter camp once, and as I was thinking about what I wanted to talk about, I was struck by this realization: *no one is going to remember what I say anyways*. How depressing is that? But at the same time, it is so true, even for me.

We sit in church on Sundays, we attend Bible studies during the week, and we go to camps and rallies to get inflamed with excitement for Jesus. But it never lasts, does it? More often than not we listen, cry, and then we return to our normal routine. How foolish can we as Christians be? James speaks directly against this saying:

> Therefore, putting aside all filthiness and all that remains of wickedness, in humility receive the word implanted, which is able to save your souls. But prove yourselves doers of the word and not merely hearers who delude themselves. For if anyone is a hearer of the word and not a doer, he is like a man who looks at his natural face in a mirror; for once he has looked at himself and gone away, he has immediately forgotten what kind of person he was.
>
> James 1:21–24

This is exactly the kind of man whom receives a great book detailing the law and how to live responsibly from the judge himself and ignores it in favor of his sexual harassment and prison time. This is exactly the kind of person the Bible demands we avoid becoming.

I find James' wording where he says, "But prove yourselves doers of the word and not merely hearers who *delude* themselves" to be amazingly poignant. How many of us have deluded ourselves in our Christian lives? How many of us hit those periods in our lives where we simply go through the motions under the belief that we are fulfilling our "Jesus" requirement of the week?

He doesn't just want us to go to church on Sunday mornings and fall asleep, he wants us to live our lives like followers of him and apply what we are taught responsibly! A church body rooted in a fear of the Lord would not be inclined to treat God as if he were the substitute teacher everyone hates. We would be active as a church, not lethargic and apathetic.

Probably my favorite comment is when people tell me they were afraid to talk to someone about Jesus. I want to say, *Oh really? Afraid of them? What about God?* And that is not to say that I am above this mentality.

Along with our salvation, and with that a real understanding of who God is, comes an enormous burden. We as Christians have this eternal truth and with that a grave responsibility from Christ himself. In his last words, he delivered what is called the Great Commission, saying:

> Go therefore and make disciples of all the nations, baptizing them in the name of the Father and the Son and the Holy Spirit, teaching them to observe all that I commanded you; and lo, I am with you always, even to the end of the age.

> Matthew 28:19–20

Our solemn duty as Christians is to deliver the gospel message to the world, but why on earth would they accept what we are offering if we don't live up to our own advertisement. You know those great commercials for all the teeth whitening strips? Don't you love how everyone's teeth in these commercials are blindingly white, and you can practically feel the cancer dripping off the enamel? (I have no idea if they actually cause cancer.) I know that they're cheesy. But who would buy the product if the commercial had a bunch of people with teeth that looked like they were smokers? "Hey all! Go out and buy our whitening so your teeth look like this!" Ummm ... no. My gut feeling tells me that very few people would go out and buy the stuff. And that makes sense, right? You don't just buy something without the promise of actual results.

As Christians, we believe in this infinitely powerful truth, this drastically life changing reality. But here's the catch: *It's supposed to be life changing.* Why is it then that so often it isn't? People will choose to dislike Christianity and religion. That's frustrating, I know. But how often will we argue with them only to have them point out all the wrongs done to them by the Church before we realize we have to start actually living like Christ in order to be effective? Who wants that teeth-whitening junk that doesn't actually work? What would be the point? And we can get frustrated, sad, and disappointed all we want, but if we aren't actually living what we as Christians say we believe, then how could we ever expect outsiders to "want what we're having"? What would be the point? Peter reminds his readers:

But even if you should suffer for the sake of righteousness, you are blessed. And do not fear their intimidation, and do not be troubled, but sanctify Christ as LORD in your hearts, always being ready to make a defense to everyone who asks you to give an account for the hope that is in you, yet with gentleness and reverence; and keep a good conscience so that in the thing in which you are slandered, those who revile your good behavior in Christ will be put to shame.

1 Peter 3:14–6

We as Christians have to remember our station here on earth. We are here to serve God's purpose. We are here for him. That's it. As Christians, we have a very specific reason for existing and continuing living. Paul said that "to live is Christ and to die is gain" in Philippians 1:21. He later writes:

To this end also we pray for you always, that our God will count you worthy of your calling, and fulfill every desire for goodness and the work of faith with power, so that the name of our LORD Jesus will be glorified in you, and you in him, according to the grace of our God and the LORD Jesus Christ.

2 Thessalonians 1:11–12

In his second letter to the Corinthians, Paul goes on to say:

> Now all these things are from God, who reconciled us to himself through Christ and gave us the ministry of reconciliation, namely, that God was in Christ reconciling the world to himself, not counting their trespasses against them, and he has committed to us the ministry of reconciliation. Therefore, we are ambassadors for Christ, as though God were making an appeal through us; we beg you on behalf of Christ, be reconciled to God.
>
> 2 Corinthians 5:18–20

Over and over again Paul emphasizes that our purpose on earth is to bring the name of Jesus Christ to anyone we can. Our station on earth is centered on glorifying Christ with our lives. In 2 Corinthians, he says that we have been "committed to … the ministry of reconciliation" by God himself and that "we are ambassadors for Christ."

How exciting is it to know that we have been chosen to represent God in a world much removed from his presence, like diplomats from a foreign nation? Yet this also carries an enormous burden because it means we must always strive to faithfully represent our nation. That is our calling, and our deeds will hinder our ultimate goal if they are not in accordance to our own standard.

Consider history for a moment. If one studies the Cold War, there are plenty of situations where ambassadors were critical to the shaping of history for all of humanity. A specific situation comes to mind. When Gorbachev came to office, Reagan invited him to visit the United States. Reagan and his men did their job and picked the best areas to take Gorbachev to visit, based on the hope that if he was impressed he might be inclined to change the ways of the "evil empire."

Now from the other perspective, Gorbachev was equally prepared. He knew that his appearance would impact how Americans saw Russia and took that very seriously, so seriously, in fact, that he wore an American brand suit that was considered very fashionable at the time. (It was specifically from Brooks Brothers, and no, I am not kidding).

Regardless, the point is clear. Both men understood the gravity of what faced them, the importance of representing their nations well. And they rose to the occasion beautifully. Together, these two were arguably the most influential players in the ending of the Cold War.

We as Christians cannot see our station any differently. We have been called to represent an almighty, holy God—a God deserving of reverent fear—to a world hurting and in the dark. We must rise to the occasion. We must behave as Christians are called to behave.

What is Love?

A third reason for this shift in perception of morality is subtler. Our understanding of love is critical to our perception of God and his justice. As a logical extension, one may ask: why is a loving God so bent on rules and regulations?

Imagine a huge family of, let's say, twelve children and the two parents. You can imagine that this house would be slightly chaotic to say the least. So to control this chaos for everyone's benefit, the father establishes rules. Now we have all been children at one point, bound by certain rules that our parents impose. We all also have likely been in one of those situations where we break the rules, cry enough to earn a "get out of jail free" card, and escape without punishment. And let's be honest, a parent who easily collapses on their rules doesn't exactly garner much respect.

Generally speaking, these parents have those lovely kids that hit their parents in public, kick and scream, and get those "I cannot believe that child is so awful" looks in the mall. So, in a way, we all know that parents who don't enforce the rules have bad kids, and life is generally less than stellar for them.

And we all also know that those kids are less equipped for a successful future. No one wants to hire a grown man who cannot take orders or submit to authority. Even if they started their own business, what kind of leader wouldn't accept advice from his employees?

But back to the lovely parents who have twelve children. Picture this household if the rules weren't enforced (any parent reading this just wept). It would be a madhouse. Babies would be flying out the windows. There would be crayon on all the walls. Someone would die, and the parents would be hoping for it (death, that is). The children would be awful; they would have no friends, and their house would be a disaster. (Call in the health department; there are cancer-causing agents here.)

Why would parents do this? Some may say it was because of love that they let the rules slip, but examining this scenario, does it really seem like they're doing the kids any favors? No! Far from it. This failure to enforce the rules is weakness, hurts his children, and as we already established, removes any chance of legitimate respect. As our good friend King Solomon said in Proverbs 13:24: "Spare the rod, spoil the child." Society thinks very poorly of a man who cannot control his children. Hopefully the point of this metaphor is also becoming clear.

In today's society, we love to feel. Everything is about how we *feel* about something, what we *want* out of something. It's a self-indulgent pattern that demands allegiance from all aspects of life and is dangerous to our currently less-than-stable theology and us.

Today's churches have adapted to this trend of "me," even if unknowingly. I want to propose that this has been done in a rather simple, seemingly harmless change. We have redefined love. Really, the definition hasn't changed that drastically, but this little change has done something destructive to the church. Love was defined previously as doing what is in the best interest of another. Love, today, I would say, has become about doing nice things for another, not expecting anything in return. Do you see the difference? The first includes this famous thing we like to call "tough love." The second lacks this aspect entirely. As a society, we do not seem to think of love as a thing that can result in an action that may hurt you. "How could you do this to me? I thought you loved me!" How many times have we thought of this or heard this? It's not an uncommon train of thought. Since we were children, we may have thought this when our parents punished us.

Love has become this soft, warm, fuzzy thing that brings light and happiness, whereas it used to be a thing of appreciation—indeed warm, but often prickly and uncomfortable. We have brought children's emotions into an everlasting God's church. Our human and finite minds have taken hold of an eternal concept that God introduced and have limited it. This understanding specifically harms our perception of living a holy life as being necessary. If we understood love, we wouldn't use it to explain why God should be submissive to our whims. It also directly impacts our ability to serve as faithful ambassadors, as our message becomes badly distorted. The havoc is nearing an irreparable point.

The parents aforementioned don't really love their children perfectly. They may indeed love their children and not like watching them suffer the consequences, but they do not love them enough to struggle through their own discomfort and punish them, knowing it is in their best interest. The parents' love could not overcome their creature comforts. God's can.

1 Kings 10:9 says, "Blessed be the Lord your God who delighted in you to set you on the throne of Israel; because the Lord loved Israel *forever*." Now that is quite the statement, right? "The Lord loved Israel forever."

Oh, but here's the funny thing. By this stage in the Bible, we had already had the whole, oh I don't know, enslavement of a nation and forty years of wandering in the desert, among other joyful stories involving thousands dead and despairing. Wait. I forgot one. He gave them the Law. This may at first glance not seem like love, and at the time the people probably didn't like God all that much at all. See, in our human minds, all this suffering and punishment couldn't possibly be the result of love.

The famous story of Job contains the moment where Job's wife comes to him, and calling on his suffering and misery (he had been scraping boils on his skin with shards of pottery), she asked, "Do you still hold fast your integrity? Curse God and die" (Job 2:9). God makes no effort to hide that people suffer in his name. He doesn't try to say that things won't be awful at times. But he sees what comes after and the blessings that will flow if you trust him to love you entirely.

Like the parent above, if you look at the bigger picture, a new clarity of vision is added. What came from the tribulations of the Israelites was far greater than the twelve sons that went into Egypt in the first place. And God seems to think the law is congruent with his love. Many in today's church will argue that God doesn't actually "like" laws and rules and that he only cares about where our hearts are at. Guess what? In Zechariah, it says this:

And I will bring the third part through the fire,
Refine them as silver is refined,
And test them as gold is tested. They will call on
My name,
And I will answer them;
I will say, "They are my people."
And they will say, "The LORD is my God."

Zechariah 13:9

His perfect love makes him perfectly pleased to refine our lives for our benefit. The Bible says this about God:

> We have come to know and have believed the love which God has for us. God is love, and the one who abides in love abides in God, and God abides in him.

1 John 4:16

God is love. This is true. This is absolutely true, and there is no denying it, no legalizing it, and no regulating it. But God is also that judge, that king, that Creator. And all his aspects are perfect, eternal, and indivisibly connected and combined. True love—God's love—is intensely interested in justice because love is truly interested in what is *best* for an individual, not what is *fun*.

As a society, we have latched onto this idea that God

is love. But we have redefined love to a much more human, much more limited perspective, and we have used it to befuddle morality and justify our mistakes. We have used the aspect of God that seemed most friendly in our terms to bring out the grey in a black and white world. We have excused ourselves. *After all, a God who wants us to be happy at all times would never expect us to follow the rules.*

But if we are honest with ourselves, we find that this is not the case. He does want us to follow the rules. *Because he loves us.* His love produces a perfect sense of justice and a perfect clarity of vision. Because he loves us, he must to maintain his standards (notwithstanding the fact that God also by nature cannot have fellowship with sin in any form). Peter asks his readers:

> For it is time for judgment to begin with the household of God; and if it begins with us first, what will be the outcome for those who do not obey the gospel of God? And if it is with difficulty that the righteous is saved, what will become of the Godless man and the sinner? Therefore, those also who suffer according to the will of God shall entrust their souls to a faithful Creator in doing what is right.
>
> 1 Peter 4:17–19

So for our benefit, our Father in heaven will enforce the rules with our punishment on earth. But just as a parent who always enforces the rules, God made one grand exception, just in the nick of time, to underscore the beauty and eternal nature of his love.

Earlier, Hebrews 10:1–4 was cited. Verses three and four say this: "But in those sacrifices there is a reminder of sins year by year. For it is impossible for the blood of bulls and goats to take away sins" (Hebrews 10:3–4). The laws we are expected to follow are rigorous, and God does not drop his standards to accommodate us. Alas, the overall punishment from breaking any law he imposes is an eternity completely separated from him.

But he knows that we cannot keep up with his standards entirely. He tells us to do so anyway. And to help wave our grand offence, he has offered himself as a sacrifice, sending his Son to die on a tree for our sins. Isaiah says this:

> But the LORD was pleased
> To crush him, putting him to grief;
> If he would render himself as a guilt offering,
> He will see his offspring,
> He will prolong his days,
> And the good pleasure of the LORD will prosper
> in his hand.
> As a result of the anguish of his soul,
> He will see it and be satisfied;

By his knowledge the Righteous one,
My Servant, will justify the many …

Isaiah 53:10–11

God loved us even in the suffering of his Son. And his sacrifice has given us an eternal pardon for our actions. But as Christians we are called to a life of holiness, and on earth, he will continue to enforce his law, for evil can never reap benefit. And above that, we are called to spread his eternal message of love like diplomats to a foreign nation, and we can never ever let our actions harm God's kingdom. After all, what kind of love is that?

A Life Worth Living

You may be asking yourself: do we actually justify ourselves? Do we really look for this grey area to explain away our faults? Yes! Look all around us. Even the news feels the need to explain things or justify them. A kidnapping or murder story always takes the time to explore the motives behind an action. When we watch, the motives don't make it "better" for us, per se, but it makes us more comfortable with it. At least it wasn't senseless … right? Often in a courtroom, certain justifications weigh heavily on the decision—insanity, to name one. We love to explain. We love to justify. And our excuses are not even necessarily public. How many of us have those secret sins, those workings of our inner heart? You alone may know them. You entertain an audience of one. Here—alone in your heart, with no judge, no jury, no reporters. And yet, we invent human explanations for our *thoughts* to defend ourselves, to make our sins "less bad" (whatever that means). If nothing else, if we can give ourselves a reason for our fall, we feel better. I know I do.

Have you ever noticed that the unexplained vice burns in your chest like a fire, simply because you cannot account for the random evil that we know is so inherently barbaric? You know if you could think of a reason of justification (oh, that word again) you would feel better. And yet, maybe you cannot. So it burns on, a daily reminder of depravity. The sins we justify somehow seem less "animalistic" simply because we gave them a human spirit. Nothing has changed once we do, we just feel better.

Think of it kind of like being trapped in a car in the desert with no air conditioning. It is way too hot, and you know there is trouble, but somehow, pouring water on your head makes you feel better inside, makes you temporarily cooler. It scares me to know that we do this so much because it reveals so completely the whole of the problem. The reality is that none of our sins are ever justified, but if we convince ourselves they are, we feel a little better. We feel less conflicted, like a man with an ulcer who takes Peptol Bismol because he initially only feels as if he has indigestion. Scary thought, isn't it?

So, do we justify ourselves? Do we look for the grey in our world to ease our indigestion? Yeah. We really do, if we are honest. If not, we just keep taking our medicine and never go to the doctor. The problem is never really fixed. And how often do we feel like that in our Christian lives? How often do we get frustrated and annoyed that we keep stumbling over the same sin? The first way to fix a problem is to acknowledge we have one. The whole world knows that. This isn't some cooked up Bible formula. This is common sense. So stop justifying!

Sometimes, and here's the tricky part, we can use the Bible to an extent and in ways it was never intended to be used. Take a look at slavery. The vast majority of early Americans thought the practice was biblically ordained. We obviously do not think so today. In a similar way, churches today have felt the need to lower our standards to accommodate the world around us in the name of making the gospel "more accessible" or more inviting. This trend of softening the message of the Bible is destructive, irresponsible, and frankly, stupid. We are damaging the message of the eternal truth our king has sent us with, and it is hurting not just us, but also nonbelievers and even society in general.

How often do we look around and despair at the condition of everything around us? We bemoan divorce rates, but we won't directly call divorce what it is. We complain about gang violence, but we don't want to stop forming "clicks" and gossiping with our associates. We hope students won't have sex before they are married, but we don't have the courage to clearly condemn the action because it could drive students away. Instead, we preach a God who *only* cares if we love him (operative word *only*). He doesn't actually care if we mess up (or so we imply). I mean, why would he?

If we as Christians expect standards, we need to be those standards. This hurting, suffering world does not need someone to tell them they aren't actually suffering. They may want that, but in all actuality, *they are*. And we have the ability and the power to tell them why. They don't need more self-help. They need total truth. I don't know why anyone would ever bother believing a religion that just gives him a backrub once a week and struggles to tiptoe around the trickier aspects of life. I know I wouldn't want to waste my time.

God loves us. He truly does. And it is amazing to know that. But he is still intensely interested in right conduct and, as such, demands this out of his church. How could we expect anything less? We are biblically called to fear God and obey his commandments. It doesn't matter if those commands are inconvenient, uncomfortable, harsh, or socially unacceptable. We are called to follow nonetheless. If nothing else, we are called to thanksgiving, and what better thanks than to show our allegiance? And if there are no changes in your life, what's the point? Why should I care about something that won't actually make a difference?

James asks similar questions: "What use is it, my brethren, if someone says he has faith but he has no works? Can that faith save him?" (James 2:14) It goes on to say:

> But someone may well say, "You have faith and I have works; show me your faith without the works, and I will show you my faith by my works." You believe that God is one. You do well; the demons also believe and shudder. But are you willing to recognize, you foolish fellow, that faith without works is useless?
>
> James 2:18–20

The Bible is clear that you are saved by grace through faith alone. Nothing you do can save you. Ever. But what you do in your life becomes important once you are saved. It isn't so much what you did before you met the Lord; it's what you do after that really counts. It will not save you. But it is a justification of your faith (in the evidence sense of the word). It's sort of like a cycle, a cycle that requires all parts. You are saved by grace through faith, which should produce a life change. These actions come about because you have this new understanding of the reality of Jesus Christ. These actions, then, justify your faith. They prove that it's really there and that it really works. It proves that customers should go out and buy your teeth-whitening product.

Think of it like a central hub to a train station. The hub is where all the tracks come from, but if there were no tracks, there would be no need for a hub, and it would shut down. Your faith will remain alive and growing if you are living in such a way. Otherwise, there's no need for your faith. It is essential as Christians that we maintain clarity of mind in regards to the nature of the moral universe, that we avoid the tragic grounds of a grey morality, for both our faith and for our world. The call is not new; it is simply a forgotten one. Jesus himself addresses this issue in his famous message in Matthew 7 about the two men who build their houses, one on rock and one on sand. He opens his story saying this:

> "Not everyone who says to Me, 'Lord, Lord,' will enter the kingdom of heaven, but he who does the will of My Father who is in heaven will enter. Many will say to Me on that day, 'Lord, Lord, did we not prophesy in Your name, and in Your name cast out demons, and in Your name perform many miracles?' And then I will declare to them,

'I never knew you; depart from me, you who practice lawlessness.'"

Do you see what he says? There will be people who labored for their entire lives under the impression that they were saved and, coming before God, will expect a ticket in. Jesus responds that he didn't know them. He calls them men who "practice lawlessness." Being a Christian is not just about knowing that Jesus is Lord. It is about having an actual faith. Can we have this and *not* attempt to become holier in God's eyes?

Jesus goes on to tell his famous story about the two houses, one on the rock and one on the sand. Unfortunately, this story has been made out to be a story about one man who is a Christian and one who is not, but in full context, it becomes clear that this is not the entire story. Both men *thought* they were Christian. The difference is that only one actually was. So, what is the difference here? The difference is that one man heard the truth and applied it. This truth really was life changing for him. It mattered.

And what of those men who encountered storms in the Bible and survived? They considered these trials as a blessing. They saw the struggles of a Christian life, the ones we have to choose to live, the difficulties of upholding the law in a flesh whose very existence is anathema to the law, as blessings to be rejoiced. The author of Hebrews seems to have had a similar idea in mind:

> Therefore, since we have so great a cloud of witnesses surrounding us, let us also lay aside every encumbrance and the sin which so easily entangles us, and let us run with endurance the race that is set before us, fixing our eyes on Jesus, the author and perfecter of faith, who for the joy set before him endured the cross, despising the shame, and has sat down at the right hand of the throne of God. For consider him who has endured such hostility by sinners against himself, so that you will not grow weary and lose heart. You have not yet resisted to the point of shedding blood in your striving against sin; and you have forgotten the exhortation which is addressed to you as sons, "My sons, do not regard lightly the discipline of the LORD, nor faint when you are reproved by him; For those whom the LORD loves he disciplines, and he scourges every son whom he receives." It is for discipline that you endure; God deals with you as with sons; for what son is there whom his father does not discipline? But if you are without discipline, of which all have become partakers, then you are illegitimate children and not sons. Furthermore, we had earthly fathers to discipline us, and we respected them; shall we not

much rather be subject to the Father of spirits, and live? For they disciplined us for a short time as seemed best to them, but he disciplines us for our good, so that we may share his holiness.

Hebrews 12:1–10

And may we share in his holiness. Wow. You see, I read that, and I don't see something worth avoiding. In fact, the passage above says we should strive for his discipline. What greater love can we find anywhere in the whole world than that expressed in Hebrews 12? This is real. This is authentic. And above all, this is love.

If I could get you to understand anything, it would be this. So, if nothing else, I pray that you read and reread the above passage until you get it. Never compromise. Never settle for less. When the curtains fall, when the lights fade, and the last member of the cast of life's drama has removed their makeup, we will be before an almighty God. Not some pushover. Not some teddy bear. God. Paul in his letter to the Romans says:

Now we know that whatever the Law says, it speaks to those who are under the Law, so that every mouth may be closed and all the world may become accountable to God; because by the works of the Law no flesh will be justified in his sight; for through the Law comes the knowledge of sin.

Romans 3:19–20

We will be silent with no excuse, no justification, no reasoning. Our mortal desires will pale before an eternal standard. As Christians, the law is our standard. Paul goes on in his letter to ask, "Do we then nullify the Law through faith? May it never be! *On the contrary, we establish the Law*" (Romans 3:31, emphasis mine). Our faith should make, if nothing else, these divine regulations even more legitimate. Our understanding of the end result of God's work should enhance our clarity of vision, not befuddle it.

The Bible provides us with a bright line. The supposed "grey" that we so eagerly hunt down is nothing but our justifications for our desires, and our success is nothing but our capitulation to our sin nature. Our post-modern society of supposed "love" has robbed us of a healthy fear of the Lord and distorted the message of Christianity, making our hunt for an excuse all the more easy.

My guess is that if this ever sees the light of public scrutiny, people everywhere will be aghast, ruffled, frustrated, and angry. I will not be surprised to be called a bigot or accused of being uncompromising or unfeeling. Here's why: in today's society we have exchanged truth for compromise. We have decided that there is no clear route to God. Everyone can be right. We have decided that there is no moral "black and white." We have as a society—and perhaps more tragically, as a church—decided that there is indeed something "beyond good and evil." I am appalled and filled with horror and dismay at this development. This couldn't be more contrary to the Gospel message!

Christianity is clear. Granted, some issues are not so obvious, but we have exchanged clear truths that *are* discernable for confusion and "tolerance." How tragic a death can our faith suffer but to die at the hands of the faithful? Has Christ died in vain?

I did not set out to write this to "legalize" Christianity. My point is not that works are the critical part of your salvation. Indeed, Paul is clear all throughout Romans that grace through faith alone can save you. I do not wish to bind Christianity to a set of rules and traditions. I wish to demand a return to Scripture. I wish to call Christians' attention to the tragic lack in moral compass we burden ourselves with in today's world.

Men will cry, "Intolerant!" I respond: No, there is no intolerance in truth. Truth is truth. How can we label truth intolerant? Is saying that someone has a broken leg intolerant because I do not allow him or her to think they are perfectly well? No! Of course not.

The entire gospel message is based on a dichotomy that has existed in nature since the garden: the dichotomy of good and evil. If you are Christian, it is critical that you believe in the difference between right and wrong. If wrong does not exist in clarity, then Christ did not have to die.

The message is clear and any undermining of it

destroys the foundation of the sacrifice we so blithely label "salvation" without stopping to think of the underpinnings of our statement. If we were saved but have no clear standards, what were we saved from? If Buddhist enlightenment could provide a road to salvation, what necessity is there in the cross? If Mormonism's works are necessary, then Christ is not enough now? How dare we as humanity attempt to transform an eternal message of clarity into a fickle message of supposed "tolerance" and "compromise"?

Humankind has sinned and fallen short of the glory of God. Therefore, we cannot be with a perfect being, lest we make him imperfect. The imperfect cannot make themselves perfect, so we depend, therefore, on God's mercy and grace, on his plan for atonement, and nothing more to be reconciled to him. If we as Christians accept compromise on any of these premises, we have bastardized the gospel message and abandoned truth for a lie. Some may be willing to do this in the name of unity. I may be called many things and criticized until the day I die, but I cannot on any grounds apologize for wanting truth, nothing more and nothing less.

As we come to a close, I want to acknowledge something: this will not be easy. Viewing the world like this will be incredibly difficult, both in how we regard our own sins and in how we interact with the world around us. People who think like this truly are outcasts.

Making a commitment towards living like this will only increase your struggles in the world. Paul says this:

> So I find this law at work: When I want to do good, evil is right there with me.
>
> Romans 7:21 (NIV)

Basically, "When I commit to doing good, evil is waiting to pounce right around the corner." It's logical, isn't it? After all, Satan and his demons could care less if you decide to live in sin. That's great! You are simply working to "bear fruit for death" (Romans 7:5). But when you commit to living as you are called, suddenly they have reason to stop you. So make no mistake: this will be massively challenging. But take heart! Peter encourages the struggling Church:

> In this you greatly rejoice, even though now for a little while, if necessary, you have been distressed by various trials, so that the proof of your faith, being more precious than gold which is perishable, even though tested by fire, may be found to result in praise and glory and honor at the revelation of Jesus Christ…
>
> 1 Peter 1:6–7

Ultimately, the benefits will far outweigh the struggles. Maybe people would actually want to be Christian.

If we live with these standards in our hearts, then more than any money we can send to Africa, more than any hours we spend in a soup kitchen, the world will actually be transformed. And who could ask for more than that?

Works Cited

""Be Still and Know That I am God"." *Contemplative (Centering) Prayer and the Cloud of Unknowing.* 10 Feb 2009 <http://www.contemplativeprayer.net/>.

Gurnall, William. *The Christian in Complete Armour Volume 1.* Carlisle, Pennsylvania: 2002.